7-8-75

11C88

FAMILIES AND THEIR CHILDREN WITH DOWN'S SYNDROME
One Feature in Common

FAMILIES AND THEIR CHILDREN WITH DOWN'S SYNDROME:

One Feature in Common

ELIZABETH A. BYRNE, CLIFF C. CUNNINGHAM
and PATRICIA SLOPER

ROUTLEDGE
London and New York

First published in 1988 by
Routledge
11 New Fetter Lane, London EC4P 4EE

Published in the USA by
Routledge
in association with Routledge, Chapman and Hall, Inc.
29 West 35th Street, New York NY 10001

**Printed and bound in Great Britain
by Billing & Sons Limited, Worcester.**

Typeset by Pat and Anne Murphy, Highcliffe-on-Sea, Dorset

British Library Cataloguing in Publication Data

Byrne, Elizabeth A.
  Families and their children with Down's
  syndrome: one feature in common.
  1. Mentally handicapped children — Family
  relationships   2. Mongolism
  I. Title   II. Cunningham, Cliff
  III. Sloper, Patricia
  362.3   HV891

ISBN 0-415-00607-4
     0-415-00608-2 (Pbk)

Library of Congress Cataloging-in-Publication Data

ISBN 0-415-00607-4
     0-415-00608-2 (Pbk)

Contents

TO THE FAMILIES
WHO HAVE BEEN OUR PARTNERS IN THIS RESEARCH
— AND TO OUR FAMILIES

Acknowledgements

It has been possible to write this book only because of the families who, for many years now, have welcomed us into their homes and their lives and shared their experiences with us. The book is dedicated to them.

The work described here has been carried out as part of the Manchester Down's Syndrome Cohort Study. All of the past and present members of the research team have contributed. We would particularly like to acknowledge Meg Aumonier, Christina Knussen, Marilyn Lawson, Chris Lennings and Ann Rangecroft. David Reeves advised and helped with the computation and statistical analyses. Professor Chris Kiernan has actively supported our work. Dr Naomi Richman acted as consultant when we were planning Study 4. Her advice and support has been appreciated.

We are grateful to Christina Knussen and Dr Margaret Flynn who provided helpful comments on earlier drafts of the manuscript. Judith Toon and Kate Catahan helped with the typing. Dr Margaret Flynn has also helped in the planning of the book and has encouraged us throughout.

The work described here has been funded largely by the Department of Health and Social Security, with some early support from the Economic and Social Research Council.

1

Perspectives on the Family

Today the family is being attacked and defended with equal vehemence. It is blamed for oppressing women, abusing children, spreading neurosis and preventing community. It is praised for upholding morality, preventing crime, maintaining order and perpetuating civilisation. Marriages are being broken more than ever before and being constituted more than ever before. The family is the place from which one desperately seeks escape and the place to which one longingly seeks refuge.

(Poster, 1978, p. ix)

For most of us, being a family member is part of our personal experience. The majority of young children grow up in families and in adulthood, many create new families. Each of us at one time or another has occupied one or more roles in a family. We are also constantly exposed to images of 'the family' through the media. Government policy presents messages about what families should and should not be doing.

Although we know from our own experience that families differ enormously from one another, the image presented is often that of one accepted model of family life — the small nuclear family of two parents and their dependent children. This image is very powerful and it lingers, despite the fact that statistically, the conventional family is no longer 'normal' (Oakley, 1982).

There is no such thing as 'the family' in the sense of one accepted model of family life. Instead, variety is the norm. Only one quarter of British households contain children. A smaller proportion still are households with a male bread-winner, a non-employed wife and dependent children.

(Graham, 1984)

Families in Britain vary in race, in their economic circumstances and in size. There may be one or two parents, and parents may or may not be married. The parents may be employed or un-employed. Some of the children in a family may be step-children, or may be fostered or adopted. Members of the extended family or others may live in the same household as the parent(s) and children. One or more family members may be ill or have a dis-ability. Despite all of this variation, the image persists of what has been called the 'cereal packet' family (Leach, 1968).

Because of the power of this image, families who differ from it may be labelled and regarded as aberrant or odd. They are likely to experience stereotyping and discrimination. For many years, researchers and practitioners regarded families of children with learning difficulties as 'pathological'. There appeared to be a genuine belief that such a child in a family would inevitably be associated with problems and would be a burden and a source of stress. This belief was reflected in the rhetoric that a child with learning difficulties meant a 'handicapped family' (Kew, 1975). Thus, researchers and practitioners assumed that all such families were similar and looked for evidence of psychological impairment in family members as a result of the child (see reviews by Byrne and Cunningham, 1985; Crnic, Friedrich and Greenberg, 1983a).

Because of this 'pathological' perspective, such research was carried out without reference to general research on families in the social sciences. This isolation meant that families of children with learning difficulties continued to be regarded as different. Impor-tant developments in how families were viewed and described had little influence on research involving families of children with learning difficulties. Similarly, developments in the ways in which services could be provided to families as a result of these changes in perspective were lost.

More recently, this view has begun to be reversed. Instead of emphasising 'pathology', research has begun to focus on the com-petence of families with children who have learning difficulties. Researchers have recognised that stressful events and experiences may have positive as well as negative consequences (Knussen and Cunningham, 1988). The difficulties experienced by families are not denied but instead, emphasis is placed both on the resources they develop in order to help them cope and on the ways in which services can complement these resources (e.g. Crnic *et al.*, 1983a; Oswin, 1984; Turnbull, Summers and Brotherson, 1986). This is the view we adopted in our research. In this book, we describe the life styles of a group of families with a child with Down's syndrome between birth and ten years of age. We discuss the families' perceptions of the impact of the child upon their lives. We show how the families differ from one another, what they have in common and how they resemble families with non-handicapped children. From this, we aim to establish the different types of needs families have and the characteristics of those families with particular needs.

We all have biases and blind spots about families, because of our own family experiences. This can influence how we treat families of children with learning difficulties in our roles as researchers, service providers and planners. Therefore, before beginning to describe the families with whom we worked and the research we carried out, it is important to be reminded of some perspectives on the family. These perspectives come from family research in different areas of the social sciences. Each has implications for services to families of children with learning difficulties (e.g. Beckman, 1984; Turnbull *et al.*, 1986; Wikler, 1986). Although most of them seem obvious, they need to be made explicit in order that, in our research, we do not merely find what we are looking for, rather than what is there.

Family variation

Families vary in who the family members are, in the number of parents and number of children included in the family, in their ethnic and cultural backgrounds, in social class and in their geographic location. A family with a particular background may have much more in common with other families from a similar background than they have with other families of children with learning difficulties. All of these factors will influence how they respond to the child, and to interventions by service personnel. For example, families belonging to a minority group may not wish to use services designed for white, middle-class families, or they may not need the same type of services (Justice, O'Connor and Warren, 1976; Stack, 1975).

Individual family members also vary in their characteristics.

Every member brings a set of personal idiosyncracies to the family and these can influence how the family reacts to the disability, how they respond to the needs of their members and how they cope with any difficulties. For example, young energetic parents, who feel in control and who have a small family, may respond enthusiastically to suggestions that they become highly involved in their child's education. Such suggestions may be the last thing that older parents, who are in poor health, or who have a large family wish to hear. They may prefer to become involved in a home-from-home scheme.

The family as a system

The family is not just a collection of individuals. It can be viewed as a system in which all of the elements interact with and influence all other elements (e.g. Turnbull *et al.*, 1986). The 'whole is more than the sum of the parts' in that the family has properties of its own over and above those of its individual members. These properties can only be understood by looking at the relationships, interactions and transactions between all members. There are also subsystems within the family system: the parental subsystem, which consists of child-parent interactions, the marital subsystem, consisting of husband – wife interactions and the sibling subsystem, consisting of child – child interactions.

Just as the individuals within a family are unique, so too are family systems. Each family varies in how close family members are to one another, how openly they communicate and how responsive the system is to change. Families have rules and habitual ways of responding to events, which are often unspoken and unacknowledged. These are brought to each family from the background and experiences of the family members. A new blend of 'ways of doing things' and 'ways of understanding and directing change' is created. Members find the skills and roles that best fit together to make the family work. These arise out of past experience and present needs. It is important for service personnel to recognise such rules in order for interventions to help the family. For example, one family member may act as a 'disagreer' who will always find reasons why interventions cannot work. This may be used to balance the perceived overenthusiasm of another family member. Unless the service provider is aware of such processes, it is unlikely that any intervention will succeed.

Like all systems, the family system has an inbuilt tendency to stability and a capacity for adaptation and growth. Anything that affects any part of the system is felt throughout the whole system. This has important implications for the provision of services to families of children with learning difficulties. Any intervention that is planned with only the child in mind, or with only the child and one parent in mind, can have unexpected and possibly harmful repercussions on other elements or subsystems within the family. For example, giving suggestions only to the mother about how to teach her child might make the child's father feel excluded, and thus cause strain on the marital subsystem. It is important to work out in advance what the likely influences on the whole system will be. A strength of this perspective is that many points of intervention into the system are possible, because of the way in which change in one part of the family system is felt throughout the whole system.

Wider systems

The family system does not function in isolation. Each family member belongs to other systems, i.e. peer group, school, work, clubs and societies. The family is embedded in a whole complex of wider systems — the extended family, friends and neighbours, educational services, the health and social services and also, the political and cultural climate. Each of these wider systems limits and determines what the family system can achieve. For example, currently, the level of unemployment is high and council housing is relatively unavailable and in a poor state of repair (Graham, 1984). This can add to the disadvantage experienced by many families of children with learning difficulties (e.g. Ineichen, 1986; Quine and Pahl, 1985). Government policy moves towards 'self-help' and voluntary help may influence the type of support available to families (Department of Health and Social Security, 1981). As Graham (1984) comments:

> Health policy in the 1980s is concerned with shifting rather than sharing responsibilities for health care. The emphasis today is less on what professionals can do for families, and more on what families, supported by voluntary efforts in the community, can do for themselves.

The extended family, friends and neighbours can provide

invaluable support to families of children with learning difficulties in terms of practical help, information and emotional support. However, they may also be a source of strain, particularly if they cannot view the child positively. They may disapprove of the family's actions, or their opinions may clash with the advice offered by professionals.

Similarly, professionals may sometimes work to the family's advantage and sometimes to their disadvantage. Often, someone from outside the family system, with good training and support from colleagues, can help a family. However, professionals from different agencies may be offering conflicting advice and support to families. Professionals may become so closely involved in the family system that they lose their clarity of vision, and may end up contributing to family difficulties. This is particularly likely when the professional has too large a caseload, few resources, and works in isolation (e.g. Dale, Davies, Morrison and Waters, 1986).

Family life cycle

No description of a family remains accurate for long. We can never feel that we fully understand a family and how it functions because families change with time. They add new members, lose members and change their roles. For example, new babies are born, children may be adopted or fostered, older children may leave home, grandparents may come to live with the family, the youngest child may become the second youngest, the father may become unemployed, a child may start school, the parents may divorce, and a new family may be constituted. All family members grow older and may be changing their beliefs and moving closer or farther apart. Interactions among members and interactions with wider systems change with time. Therefore, the family life cycle encompasses more than the sum of the life cycles of individual family members.

At different stages in the family life cycle, different tasks have to be accomplished. Family needs vary according to their stage in the lifecycle. Whereas it may be appropriate, for example, for the parents of young children to be closely involved in teaching their children at home, the parents of adolescents may wish to encourage them to attend youth clubs and extend their social contacts. Similarly, activities that are appropriate for families with young children, such as outings to the park or the beach, or family

6

holidays, may be less appropriate as the children reach adolescence, when separate outings or holidays may be enjoyed more by all family members.

The family system can be resistant to change. Change is frequently associated with uncertainty and upheaval. Energy is needed to cope with this uncertainty, with the need to make decisions and establish new routines. Often, older members are more resistant, while younger ones push for change. The changes that occur during the transition from one stage to another in the family lifecycle may cause uncertainty and anxiety. It is during these transitions that families may be most in need of help from service personnel, for example, when children with learning difficulties start school, reach puberty, or leave school (Wikler, 1986). Yet often, the transitions involve changes in the personnel who have contact with the family, e.g. from preschool to school staff. Transitions involving other family members or the entire family may also cause anxiety, for example, when siblings leave home or when parents retire. Paradoxically, it is during such transitions that the family system is most open to change because of the disorganisation, confusion and increases in energy that occur at this time. Where family members wish to change habitual patterns that they feel are unhelpful, this is often the best time to try (Hoffman, 1981).

Summary

This chapter serves as a reminder that the 'cereal packet' image (Leach, 1968) of the family does not correspond to the structure of most British families. This image continues to have a powerful effect, and can influence how, as researchers, policy makers, service providers and family members, we treat families who vary from it. In order to provide a service to families of children with learning diffculties, we need to remember that:

— as far as family structure in Britain is concerned, variety is the norm and families of children with learning difficulties vary as much as do all families;

— families of children with learning difficulties may also belong to other groups of families, e.g. single-parent families, families in poverty, families in ethnic minorities. As members of such groups they share characteristics in common with other members. They also have characteristics in common with all families, characteristics that are unique to each family and characteristics that they share with other families of children with learning difficulties;

— families are not just collections of individuals. The family is a transactional system in which all family members interact with and influence all other members. Anything that influences one part of the system is felt throughout the whole system;

— the family system does not exist in isolation. It is influenced by and exerts influence upon the wider systems of which it is a part, i.e. social networks, services and political and cultural regimes. These wider systems can limit or enhance the family's effectiveness and the effectiveness of any interventions;

— families change over time. Interventions that are appropriate at one stage may not be appropriate at a later stage, and we can never assume that we fully 'understand' a family.

In the remainder of this book, we describe some of the research we carried out with a group of families who each have a young child with Down's syndrome. We discuss the mothers' perceptions of the impact of the children upon their lives and the lives of their families. We show how the families differ from one another, what they have in common and how they resemble families with non-handicapped children. From this, we describe the different needs that different families have.

2
The Manchester Down's Syndrome Cohort Study

The white paper entitled 'Better services for the mentally handicapped' (DHSS, 1971) stated as a general principle that: 'Each handicapped person should live with his own family as long as this does not impose an undue burden on them or him, and he and his family should receive full advice and support.' Sixteen years later, the advice and support that families require has not yet been satisfactorily clarified. In 'Mental handicap: progress, problems and priorities' (DHSS, 1980) it was concluded that further work was required on 'the roles of the various professionals who provide services to families of mentally handicapped children', on 'service policy' and on 'how services to families can best be co-ordinated'.

Although such desires are commonly expressed, there is insufficient information available about what the needs of families of children with learning difficulties are. Indeed, many such reports and advisory documents appear to stereotype families of children with learning difficulties and assume that they all have similar needs and that we know what those needs are and can meet them.

It was this realisation that led us to the research described in this book. We had been engaged in research on early development, family support and intervention with a cohort of 181 families who each had a child with Down's syndrome born in Greater Manchester between August 1973 and August 1980 (The Manchester Down's Syndrome Cohort). During our many discussions with the parents, a large number of issues began to emerge. Some families appeared to be experiencing difficulties, describing relationship problems, difficulties with the children and feelings of restriction and isolation. Others spoke of their concerns about the services they received, or about the reactions of others to themselves and their children. For many, future provision for their children was a frequently expressed worry. On the other hand, some families did not recount concerns, but told of their unexpected delight in the child. The question that has engaged us since is 'why?' What is it about some families that enables them to cope successfully, and why do other families experience such difficulties?

It was from this starting point that we decided to embark on a series of comprehensive interview studies. The aims were: to discover the perspectives of the parents themselves, to describe their different concerns, to explore the differences among families with a child with Down's syndrome and to examine some of the possible reasons for these differences. The rest of this chapter describes the background to this research and the families who took part in it.

The Manchester Down's Syndrome Cohort Study

The Manchester Down's Syndrome Cohort Study began in 1973, when local paediatricians were contacted and asked to refer all recently born infants for whom a diagnosis of Down's syndrome had been made. The broad aim of the research, at that time, was to investigate the development of infants with Down's syndrome and the particular factors that influence the course of development, including the type of early stimulation and care they received. Those families who were referred, and who wished to be involved received a home-based, early intervention service.

At first, referrals were sparse and irregular. However, as the research became better known, and those who received the early intervention fed back positive comments to services, the referral rate increased rapidly. Initially, paediatricians made most referrals but in late 1976, health visitors were also contacted and asked to refer families. Families could also refer themselves. From 1976 until 1980, over 90 per cent of all infants with Down's syndrome, born in the ten area health authorities of Greater Manchester were referred. In all, 203 referrals were received, and of these, 181 families were included in the study and formed the cohort.

Many different research studies have been carried out, using all or some of the families as participants. Some of these studies were related directly to the method and content of the early intervention programme. Others were broader in perspective and were related to family or service issues. For the first few years of the childrens' lives, the research centred around a home-visiting and intervention programme that minimally included:

(1) One or more 'first' visits as soon as possible after the family had been referred to the project.
(2) Regular six-weekly home visits from 6 weeks of age until 78 weeks of age, which incorporated assessment, support, and advice on stimulation.
(3) Home visits at 12-weekly intervals until 2 years of age. During these visits the support and advice was continued, but parents were also encouraged to begin to seek out other services such as playgroups, opportunity groups or schools.
(4) Home visits at six-monthly intervals until five years of age.

During these visits, follow-up developmental data was collected, issues of concern to parents were discussed and guidance was offered when requested. Throughout these five years, all parents were repeatedly told that they could contact members of the research team at any time for consultation or discussion.

Research philosophy and method

The early-intervention service developed in response to the needs and demands of the parents. Our philosophy was that the researchers and parents were partners in their endeavour to ensure that the infant was provided with every opportunity to develop. The parents were seen as partners who had close and continuing contact with their own child, and therefore had expert knowledge about that child. The researchers brought to the partnership knowledge about Down's syndrome and about developmental processes from their contact with many children (Cunningham, 1983a).

Thus, all our research is based upon the conviction that we learn more from families when they are active participants in the research, rather than mere sources of data. Our approach has always been to regard the parents as 'consumers'. The team offered parents any information that was likely to be necessary for them to live with and help their own child, themselves and other family members. The parents were free to select from this in their own way, in their own time and according to their needs at that time. This approach, as is implied by a 'consumer – partnership model' (Cunningham and Davis, 1985a), gives the parent responsibility for acquiring the information and skills needed for themselves and their children.

The research had to be longitudinal in order to move with the needs of families and children and investigate the development of the child. It also had to be 'reactive' and responsive to the changing needs of families. It had to take account of the many factors that influence children and families. Such factors included: the characteristics of individuals within the family and of the family as a unit; resources possessed by individual family members, i.e. health and problem-solving skills; relationships within the family; the family's social and support networks; and the political and socio-cultural environment of the family (Bronfenbrenner, 1977).

The studies

In this book we mainly describe the findings of four interview studies that were conducted separately and did not always include all families. However, they were all bound by common themes and objectives. In later chapters, we have blended the results and wherever possible traced effects over time for those families who took part in more than one study. In order to give an overview, we will briefly outline each study below.

Study 1: Diagnosis and early family needs

One of the first observations made in the course of early visits to the families was that parents usually described how they were told of the diagnosis of Down's syndrome. Their descriptions were often vivid and emotional. They frequently included statements of dissatisfaction and anger towards those who had told them of the diagnosis. It was clear that the way in which parents were told that their infant had Down's syndrome often had a profound effect on them. It also appeared that the way they were told might affect how they adjusted to the situation, and how they interacted with their baby. These observations confirmed many previous interview studies in Britain (e.g. Berg, Gilderdale and Way, 1969; Carr, 1970; Drillien and Wilkinson, 1964) and in America (e.g.

Gayton and Walker, 1974; Pueschel and Murphy, 1976).

As a result, 30 families from the cohort were interviewed soon after they had been told of the diagnosis (Cunningham and Sloper, 1977a). Parents were encouraged to describe how and when they were told, and their descriptions were categorised in terms of the following questions derived from Carr (1970): (1) When were parents told? (2) Did they have any suspicions about the baby before being told, and why? (3) How were they told? (4) What did they recall from this first interview? (5) Was there access to further information and assistance? (6) What do parents want from these early interviews? (7) Do parents seek second opinions? (8) How long does it take to get over the initial shock? A further survey of 59 parents in the cohort was carried out 3 years later (Cunningham, Morgan and McGucken, 1984), in order to see whether the research literature and feedback through talks to professional meetings had influenced practice and in turn, parental satisfaction.

The next step was to test whether parental dissatisfaction with the way in which they were told was inevitable. To do this, an 'ideal' service was set up, based both on the literature and on the results of our previous studies. The paediatricians and health visitors in one area health authority included in the interview studies approached us for information on how to improve their services. In collaboration with us, the paediatrician and a specialist health visitor (who had been trained by our team) then developed a policy whereby certain guidelines were followed when parents were being told of the diagnosis and during the follow-up period. Nine families who received this service were compared to 25 families from other area health authorities who formed a contemporary control group. Similar questions were asked to those in the previous studies. The findings of this series of studies are described chiefly in Chapter 9.

Study 2: Views about school

Rapoport, Rapoport and Strelitz (1977) suggest that families are potentially subject to strain at 'normal' transition points — the birth of a child, children entering school, children leaving home. It has also been suggested that such transitions are likely to cause greater difficulties for families of children with learning difficulties (Wickler, Wasow and Hatfield, 1981). We quickly became aware of parental concerns about the transition to school because of requests for information and guidance as the child reached pre-school, and later, school age. Parents were concerned about which type of school would be best for the child, when the child should start school, and what their own role would be in relation to the child's education.

In response to these concerns, Study 2 set out to interview all of those families whose children were five years of age or older about issues concerned with schooling. The aim was to describe the processes involved in the child's transition to school, to describe school life as viewed by the mother, and within this, to examine areas where problems may arise. The interview covered: preschool placement; details of school attended and transition to school; assessment; choice of placement; mothers' involvement in school; parent and child satisfaction; problems encountered; child friendships; mothers' contact with others; integration; and parental aspirations for the child. The interviews of Gregory (1970), Hewett (1970) and Newson, Newson and Barnes (1977) were used as guides in constructing the interview schedule.

The mothers of all children in the cohort who were five years of age or older, and who had been at school for at least two terms were contacted and asked to participate in this study. Of the 67 families who fulfilled these criteria, 60 mothers were interviewed at home. The seven families who were not included did not differ in any consistent way from those who participated. The findings of this study are presented and discussed chiefly in Chapters 3 and 9.

Study 3: The child, the family and the community

Unlike Studies 1 and 2, which deal with particular events in the family life cycle, the aim of Study 3 was to provide an overview of all of the families in the cohort and of all of the issues that concerned them at the time. We wanted to find out what differentiated those families who expressed distress and unhappiness from those who appeared to have no concerns. The ages of the children ranged from two to ten years at the time of the study, and families were therefore at different stages in their life cycles.

At the time of this study, there were 134 families remaining in the cohort. Attrition was due to deaths of the children and to families moving away. One hundred and twenty four families, i.e. 93 per cent of those remaining in the cohort, were included in this study. The distribution of this sample did not differ in any consistent way from that of the entire original cohort. The interviews with the mothers took place in the family home. The issues covered were those that had been raised during follow-up visits to families, and those that the research literature suggested were important. These were: the child's activities and relationships with friends and siblings; the child's relationship with the parents; nuclear family interrelationships and activities; relationships with the extended family, friends and neighbours; relationships with health, educational and social services; and maternal values and aspirations.

The work of Carr (1975), Gath (1978), Waisbren (1980), Wilkin (1979), Wing and Gould (1978) and Wishart, Bidder and Gray (1981) provided guidelines for the design of the interview and the topics included. The social ability of the children was assessed as part of the interview using the Vineland Scale of Social Maturity (Doll, 1965). Mothers were also asked to complete the Malaise Inventory (Rutter, Tizard and Whitmore, 1970) in order to measure how stressful they found their situation. The findings of this study are described throughout the book.

Study 4: Family relationships and the children's behaviour

Information from informal contact with the families, from the findings of Study 3 and from the research literature combined to suggest that the behaviour of their children with Down's syndrome was an important source of concern to many families. Study 4 was set up in order to examine this area more thoroughly. The aim of the study was: to investigate the factors associated with behaviour difficulties in children with Down's syndrome between five and ten years of age. Such factors include child, parent and family characteristics, and physical and social characteristics of the family environment (Gibson, 1978; Quine, 1986; Richman, Stevenson and Graham, 1982). One of the purposes of the study was to evaluate any long-term effects of the early intervention on behaviour difficulties.

The study compared 60 cohort children aged five to ten years with 60 children who had not received early intervention from the research team. The children were matched on age, sex and social class and lived in or on the outskirts of Greater Manchester. The characteristics of the areas of residence were similar in both groups. Each child was assessed once in school and each mother was interviewed once at home. The interviews covered background and demographic details, family interrelationships, informal and formal support, family social contacts and outings, caretaking and supervisory demands, stressful events, child management practices, child health, child activities and contacts. A major portion of the interview was devoted to behaviour problems. To provide a comparison with a non-handicapped group of children, many of the measures devised by Richman *et al.* (1982) were used.

In addition to the interview questions, mothers were asked to complete several written checklists and scales. These were (1) a checklist of the child's self-help and adaptive skills; (2) the Malaise Inventory (as used in Study 3); (3) the Judson Self Rating Scale (Judson and Burden, 1980), devised as a measure of parental adjustment to the child's disability; (4) the Behaviour Checklist (Richman *et al.*, 1982) to assess behaviour problems in siblings under 6 years of age and the Rutter Scale A (Rutter *et al.*, 1970) for those aged six to 16. The Judson scale was also left for completion by fathers. Following the interview, the interviewer discussed the results of the child's assessments with the mother. The findings of this study are also presented throughout the book.

Using interviews to gather information

Interviews were used to gather information in all of the studies described here. In each case, the interviewing technique was similar. Interviews were semi-structured and the wording and ordering of questions was set down on a schedule. Written prompts were also provided. However, the interviewers (who were also the researchers) could vary slightly from the wording and from the order of questions in order to maintain the flow of conversation. In the early stages of each study, two interviewers visited the home. One conducted the interview and both noted and coded replies. They alternated roles for different interviews. Using this procedure, percentage agreement between the two interviewers was over 90 per cent for all sections of the interviews. It is worthwhile spending some time considering the strengths and weaknesses of this technique and the validity of the data produced.

The data that results from interviews consists of the views and perceptions of the person interviewed. It is arguable whether these would correspond to the perceptions of other family members, or to people outside the family, or indeed, to observations made by a researcher. However, this does not mean that the perceptions of individual family members are not important and valid sources of data, especially when one of the aims of the research is to make recommendations for service provision to families. A number of studies have found that stress experienced by mothers of children with learning difficulties is more closely related to subjective factors than to directly measurable features (Beckman, 1983; Bradshaw and Lawton, 1978). For example, Bradshaw (1980) found that Malaise scores were related to satisfaction with housing but not to actual housing standards.

The information presented in the book consists of the views of the mothers in the cohort. During the interviews, we asked mothers for their views of the effect of the child with Down's syndrome on themselves and their lives. We also asked them how they thought their husbands, any other children, and the wider family had been affected. We asked them to describe the relationship between the child and his/her brothers and sisters. We are aware that mothers' views may be quite different to those of siblings or fathers, and feel strongly that the views of all family members should be sought. Indeed, in Study 4, we found no relationship between mothers' descriptions of fathers' relationships with the children and fathers' own perceptions of their relationships with their children measured by the Judson Scale. For this reason, fathers are being interviewed in our current research study. However, as mothers spend most time with their young children, attend to most of their needs and are most likely to deal with service providers, we felt that it was most important to ask their views first (Cockburn, 1977). As the principal carer, the mother is the direct consumer and mediator of services:

> Normally, and by preference, the state deals not with individuals but with *families*. More often than not it deals with the *woman* of the family. Who answers the door when the social worker calls? Who talks to the head teacher about the truant child? Who runs down to the rent office? The woman, wife and mother.
>
> (Cockburn, 1977, p. 58)

Given that the views and perceptions of family members are valuable sources of data, we must now consider to what extent our interview data represents these views in a reliable and valid way.

When the aim of the research is to explore differences between individuals, it is possible that some of the differences in what people say may be related to differences in their use of language, e.g. how articulate and eloquent they are, or to differences in what they are prepared to say, e.g. whether they feel that what they do is socially acceptable or not. Newson and Newson (1963) found that mothers of one-year-old children described their child-rearing practices differently to health visitors and to university interviewers. We used a number of different techniques to overcome these potential problems.

Firstly, all interviewers were part of the research team. The relationship between the team and the families in the cohort had developed over many years, and was largely one of equality and mutual respect (Cunningham, 1983a). Throughout all interactions with parents, every opportunity was taken to explain that their perceptions and observations as partners in the research enterprise were needed and highly valued. We emphasised the importance of information about what went wrong, as well as what went well. We hope that our relationship with parents was such that they could comment freely, and know that demands would be met as far as possible. Thus, the context in which the interviews took place was different to many interview studies in which the interviewer meets those interviewed once only.

Secondly, where we were asking questions about events and behaviour, rather than views, the questions were specific and neutral, and not open to alternative interpretations. Thirdly, a response to one question was rarely taken on its own, but was combined with the responses to other questions on a similar theme. In Study 4, ratings were made, not just on responses to questions, but also on non-verbal indications, for example facial expression, tone of voice, loudness, gestures, etc. This technique was adapted from the work of Brown and Rutter (1966), who describe its reliability and validity.

The main alternatives to interviewing are questionnaires, rating scales and attitude inventories. We felt these were inappropriate for three main reasons. Firstly, they did not cover all of the areas we wished to include. Secondly, it is difficult to select appropriately standardised instruments. Finally, as Newson and Newson (1976a) argue, the use of such instruments means that:

> often the status of the individual as a thinking person, with the possibility both of making his own insights and of

voluntarily supplying material which will allow others to make insights, seems to be mislaid on the way.

We felt that given our relationship of equality with the families, they should be the informants about their own lives. It is only through interviews that one gains information both about events and, of equal importance, about people's feelings associated with those events.

The families

It is difficult to know how to describe the families in the cohort because, like all families, they are changing continually. In this section, they will be described as they were at a single point in time. The time chosen was the time of Study 3 (when the children were between two and ten years old) because this study includes the greatest number of cohort families and is discussed most fully in the book.

The characteristics of the children and their families are presented in Tables 2.1 and 2.2 respectively. In the case of children who were adopted or fostered, the figures refer to their foster or adoptive families. There are more boys than girls in the cohort

Table 2.1: Child characteristics

Age	2:5 – 3:6	3:7 – 4:6	4:7 – 5:6	5:7 – 6:6	6:7 – 9:11
%	29	20	23	11	16
Sex		Male		Female	
%		61		39	
Placement		Natural parents		Fostered/adopted	
%		94		6	
Position in family	Only child	Youngest		Oldest	Middle
%	10	53		18	19
Medical problems	Severe problem(s)		Minor problem(s)		No problem(s)
%	32		38		30
Social quotient[a]	20 – 50	51 – 60	61 – 70	70 +	Missing
%	11	23	31	23	12
Social age	0 – 2:0	2:1 – 3:0	3:1 – 4:6	4:7 – 7:0	Missing
%	21	31	25	11	12

Note: a. Social age is derived from the Vineland scale of social maturity (Doll, 1965) and the method for calculating social quotient is equivalent to that for calculating IQ i.e. Soc Age/C. Age × 100.

Table 2.2: Parent and family characteristics

Marital status	Married (1st marriage)		Married (2nd marriage)		Single
%	81		15		4
Mean parental age at birth of child	15 – 24	25 – 29	30 – 34	35 +	Not known
%	19	19	32	27	2
Parent's education[a]	1	2	3		Missing
%	27	31	38		4
Father's employment	Not Working		Working		No father
%	8		88		4
Mother's employment	Not working		Part-time		Full-time
%	56		38		6
Social class	I + II		III		IV + V
%	40		41		19
Number of children	1	2	3		4 +
%	10	39	30		21
Religion	C of E	RC	Other		No religion
%	52	25	11		12
House ownership	Own house		Council/rented		Not known
%	68		31		1

Notes: a. 1. Neither parent has further education (i.e. post 16 years)
2. One parent has further education
3. Both parents have further education

(Cunningham, 1983b). This difference may reflect the higher mortality rate found in female infants with Down's syndrome (e.g. Cowie, 1970). There are also more families from social classes I and II (i.e. families in which the main wage earner is a professional) than in the general population. Again, this has been reported in other British studies of children with Down's syndrome (e.g. Carr, 1970; Ludlow and Allen, 1979; Gath, 1978). This discrepancy could be due to the greater incidence of perinatal and infant mortality in social classes IV and V (Graham, 1984). Another factor that may contribute to the discrepancy is that women from social classes I and II are older when they have their children (Osborn, Butler and Morris, 1984). They are therefore more likely to give birth to a child with Down's syndrome (Cunningham, 1987).

The medical problems described by mothers and the percentage of children with each problem are presented in Table 2.3. Medical

Table 2.3: Medical problems

Problem	% of children
Severe cardiac problem	22
Minor cardiac problem	32
Blind or partially sighted	1
Deaf or partially hearing	22
Requires spectacles	33
Slight conductive hearing loss	33
Slightly impaired mobility	3
Epilepsy/fits	6
Other	6
No problems	30

problems categorised as severe in Table 2.1 include severe cardiac problems, partial sight or blindness, partial hearing or deafness and epilepsy.

Tables 2.1 and 2.2 demonstrate the heterogeneity of the families in the cohort. Having a child with Down's syndrome as a family member is the only feature that they all possess in common. As Table 2.1 demonstrates, the children with Down's syndrome are also a varied and diverse group. It is worth remembering, when considering the lifestyles of these children and their families, that, at the time of the interview, many of them were coping with at least one major source of potential stress or concern in addition to their child's disability. Thirty-two per cent of the children lived with severe medical problems, which almost inevitably affected them and their families. Similarly, in 16 per cent of families, a sibling had a medical problem. Examples of such problems include cerebral palsy, which resulted in impaired mobility, arthritis, asthma, and cleft lip and palate. In six per cent of the families, a child had died before the birth of the child with Down's syndrome. In eight per cent, the fathers were unemployed and the families were coping with the stress that can result from unemployment as well as with reduced financial circumstances. Four per cent were single-parent families and in 15 per cent of families, the marriage was a second one for one or both partners. Thirty-nine per cent of the families experienced at least one of these potential sources of stress and 13 per cent, more than one.

With regard to material circumstances, 19 per cent of families did not have a car, 14 per cent had no phone, four per cent lived in houses that had neither a garden nor yard in which the children could play, three per cent lived in council flats and, twelve per cent of families were dissatisfied with their housing. Twenty-three per cent of families were affected by one of these latter features and 15 per cent by more than one.

It is relevant to compare some of the frequency distributions shown in Tables 2.1 and 2.2 with those from other concurrent studies of families. It is difficult, however, to know which studies to use for the purposes of comparison. We have chosen to use two sources: statistics applying to all families in Britain at the time of Study 3 (Central Statistical Office, 1984); and a study of all families of children with severe learning difficulties in Kent (Quine and Pahl, 1985). The bias towards social classes I and II in the cohort families will influence any comparison and must be borne in mind. Also, the families in the cohort are not directly comparable to those in the study by Quine and Pahl (1985). Not all of the children in their study had Down's syndrome, and not all of the children in our study had severe learning difficulties. Many showed moderate or mild learning difficulties. Also, the age range of the children included in Quine and Pahl's study was much greater, ranging from birth to 16 years of age. We hope that using both sources together will provide useful comparisons.

In 1982/83 when this data was collected, national figures showed that 13 per cent of families with dependent children were single-parent families (Central Statistical Office, 1984). Among the families of children with severe learning difficulties in Kent, a similar proportion were single-parent families (Quine and Pahl, 1985). Reference to Table 2.2 shows that in this study, the proportion of single-parent families was much smaller (four per cent). Two factors probably contribute towards this lower frequency: the relatively young ages of the children, and the greater proportion of families from social classes I and II.

The unemployment rate for men in the United Kingdom was 13 per cent in 1983 (Central Statistical Office, 1984). A similar proportion of fathers of children with severe learning difficulties in Kent were unemployed (Quine and Pahl, 1985). The figure of eight per cent for the families in the Manchester cohort compares favourably with this (see Table 2.2), and is also likely to be due to the bias towards social classes I and II in the cohort families.

As far as the mothers were concerned, six per cent were in full-time paid employment, a similar proportion to that noted by Pahl and Quine (1984). However, many more mothers were in part-time paid employment (38 per cent) than those reported by Pahl and Quine (1984), where the figure is 26 per cent. This was at a time when 9.5 per cent of mothers of children under the age of nine were in full-time paid employment and 33.5 per cent were in part-time paid employment (Central Statistical Office, 1984). In 1984/85 when Study 4 was carried out, including only the mothers of older children (five to ten years), 57 per cent were in paid employment, a figure similar to the national figures for mothers in the same age range. More mothers in the cohort were in paid employment than the mothers in the comparison group. There is therefore some evidence that in the families who received early intervention, mothers may have been more likely to take employment.

In terms of house ownership, 68 per cent of the families in Study 3 owned their own house. This is similar to the figures for Britain as a whole — 67 per cent (Central Statistical Office, 1984) and very slightly higher than that reported by Pahl and Quine (1984) — 63 per cent. The figures for possession of cars and telephones are much higher than the average for British households with young children (Central Statistical Office, 1984) and probably reflect the social-class bias in the cohort.

These figures indicate that patterns of house ownership and maternal employment are similar for the families considered here and families in Great Britain generally. With regard to paternal employment, less men were unemployed than the national figures suggest. Once again, it is important to remember, that more of the families described here belong to social classes I and II and that the proportion of single-parent families is much smaller than in the UK as a whole.

Summary

This chapter sets the scene for the remainder of the book. It traces the development of the Manchester Down's Syndrome Cohort Study, outlining the overall research philosophy and method. It describes the four research studies that are the focus of the book, shows how these developed from the main study and discusses the use of interviews as a way of gathering information. Finally, it describes the families who took part in the studies. With the exception of a bias towards social classes I and II, these are similar to families in Britain at the time of the studies.

The research attempted to take account of the many factors that influence children and their families. In particular, we tried to understand how the families are different from one another and why some of them experience difficulties. We hope the following chapters go some way towards providing a picture of the movement of ordinary life for the families in the Manchester Down's Syndrome Cohort and for other families of children with learning difficulties.

3

The Children: their Activities, Friends, Sisters and Brothers

In this chapter, we describe how the children in the cohort spend their days — the schools and preschools they attend; the clubs and classes in which they are involved outside school; the toys and activities they enjoy; and their relationships with friends, sisters and brothers.

We were interested in the children's day-to-day lives for three reasons. It is easy to stereotype children with Down's syndrome, to regard them just as a 'worry', and a 'burden', or as 'passive' and 'easy'. All children have busy and varied lives. They occupy numerous different roles both within and outside the family (Lewis, Feiring and Kotsonis, 1984), e.g. pupil, friend, sister or brother, cub or brownie. They spend their time busily engaged in activities that they may share with others or that may be quite private (Davie, Hutt, Vincent and Mason, 1984). They have favourite activities and activities they dislike. We wanted to explore this variety for the children in the cohort: to find out how they differ from one another and what they share in common with one another and with groups of non-handicapped children.

Secondly, we were aware that the day-to-day life of the families, which we explore in later chapters, was dependent to some extent on the day-to-day life of their children. If children can be left alone to amuse themselves or if they play happily with other children, then their mothers may have more free time. If they attend a local playgroup or school, or 'play out' on the street with others, their parents may meet other parents and feel part of a community. When young children are delayed in moving through developmental milestones or when younger siblings overtake them, the movement of the family through its lifecycle may be delayed or altered (Turnbull *et al.*, 1986).

Finally, we wished to describe any difficulties experienced by the children or their families in these areas, and to find out which children and families experienced such difficulties. From these explorations, we hoped to be able to indicate which families might be vulnerable and to offer suggestions as to how their needs could be met.

Presentation of findings

In this and in subsequent chapters, the findings from the four interview studies described in Chapter 2 will be presented in a number of different ways. Firstly, in order to indicate differences and similarities among the families, we give details of the range of different answers given to specific questions and the proportions answering in each way. These frequencies are illustrated and amplified by quotations from the interviews. Where possible, comparisons are made with other interview studies of families of children with and without disabilities. In this context, the work of Newson and Newson (1968; 1976b; 1977) is referred to frequently. Although these interview studies were carried out many years ago, there are no comparable current studies that provide the same richness of longitudinal detail from a large and representative sample of British families.

Secondly, differences between subgroups of the cohort are presented, e.g. differences according to social class, age of child, health of child, type of school attended, etc. Only differences that are statistically significant are included. The statistical tests that we used are described in the appendix.

Finally, in order to identify which children and families are vulnerable and the factors associated with such vulnerability, the findings of a series of multivariate analyses are presented. We derived a number of measures of outcome from the interview data. Some of these measures are positive, e.g. 'maternal satisfaction', and some negative e.g. 'child-behaviour problems'. They reflect outcomes for different family members, e.g. 'sibling relationships', 'maternal stress'.

The measures were arrived at by combining together all of the answers given by mothers on particular themes in the interview. For example, the measure called 'child's friends and play' consists of all the information on this topic for each child. We examined the relationship between each child, parent and family characteristic and the different outcome measures, using analyses of variance. The type of analyses that we used is also described in the appendix.

The children's activities

Over 95 per cent of the children under five years of age were attending a preschool facility at the time of Study 3. Thirty-eight per cent attended some type of mainstream facility, 17 per cent an integrated facility and 45 per cent a special facility (see Table 3.1). Eighty-two per cent of this group of children under five attended

Table 3.1: Types of preschool facilities attended

	% attending
Mainstream facilities	
Nursery class/school	14
Day nursery	9
Playgroup	6
Mother–toddler group	9
Integrated facilities	
Integrated playgroup	10
Special nursery in mainstream school	1
Child opportunity group	6
Special facilities	
Nursery class in special school	37
Special nursery school	7
Special playgroup	1

a facility where they were left by their mothers. This is a higher percentage than has been found for non-handicapped children. The national longitudinal study of children born during one week in April 1970 in Britain (Osborn *et al.*, 1984) found that only 72 per cent of children had some preschool experience. This difference is possibly due to changes in the pattern of attendance at preschool with time. The policy of special schools of accepting children into their nursery classes from the age of two may also contribute to the different rates of attendance.

It is clear from the work of Armstrong, Jones, Race and Ruddock (1980) that there are large regional differences both in the proportion of children with learning difficulties who attend preschool facilities, and in the types of facilities available. More of the children who formed our cohort attended preschool and they attended a greater variety of provisions than in other British urban areas (Armstrong *et al.*, 1980). As with other aspects of service provision, where families live is important in determining the quality and variety of services available to them (Plank, 1982). This does not just depend on the availability of a variety of different provisions. Families require information about what is available and advice and support in making their decisions. For example, when we compared children from the cohort with those who had not received our early intervention service, we found that the cohort children were more likely to have attended a mainstream preschool setting. There were no major differences in the children's abilities or in family location. It seems that the support and information that the intervention provided enabled families to seek out a placement in an ordinary preschool setting for their children.

Of the children who were five years of age or more, ten per cent attended a mainstream school, eight per cent a special unit in a mainstream school and 82 per cent a special school. The types of school facilities attended are listed in Table 3.2. Over half of the children under five (55 per cent) had the opportunity to interact with non-handicapped children at their preschool, whereas only 18 per cent of school age children had such an opportunity at school.

Table 3.2: Types of school facilities attended

Facility	% attending
Mainstream class	10
Special class/unit in mainstream school	8
School for children with moderate learning difficulties	13
School for children with severe learning difficulties	68

Apart from school, 35 (28 per cent) of the children attended a club or class (Table 3.3). Some of these children attended many classes. For example, one seven-year-old girl had ballet, ballroom and tap dancing and piano lessons. Another nine-year-old belonged to a Morris Dancing troupe. One nine-year-old boy attended Sunday school, cubs, a gymnastic club and had cornet lessons. Older children (i.e. from five to ten years) were significantly more likely than younger children to attend clubs or classes. Of those 82 children not attending any clubs or classes, 62 mothers said that they intended enrolling their children when they were

Table 3.3: Clubs and classes attended

Club/class	% attending
Sunday school	12
Sport (e.g. swimming, gymnastic classes)	8
Dancing classes	6
Cubs/Brownies	3
Special club (e.g. Gateway)	9

older. The children's gender, social ability or health was not found to be related to their attendance at clubs or classes.

We now move on to consider the children's activities at home and in their immediate neighbourhoods:

> To the four year old, play is a serious and absorbing activity. Through it, he discovers many exciting new experiences, develops and practises a personal repertoire of new skills, and explores a fascinating world of new sensations, new materials and new situations.
>
> (Newson and Newson, 1968, p. 173)

The types of activity noted by parents in our study are very similar to those described by Davie *et al.* (1984) in their observational study of three- to five-year-old children. In their study, children spent most time engaged in watching television, gross motor activites, pretend play and looking at books. These activities were cited most often by the mothers we interviewed in response to such questions as 'What does your child like doing best?' (Table 3.4) and 'What does he/she play?' (Table 3.5).

Both Newson and Newson (1968) and Davie *et al.* (1984) emphasise the predominance of fantasy and pretend play in the

Table 3.4: Favourite activities

Activities	% of children
Playing (see Table 3.5)	61
Watching TV	26
Being with other people	18
Music	15
Playing outside	12
Helping parents	10
Exploring	7
Being destructive	7
Eating	5
Physical activity	3
Outings with family	2

Table 3.5: The children's play activities at home

Play	% of children	
	Alone	With friends
Object play (dolls, cars, etc.)	48	48
Looking at books	45	8
Pretend play	37	48
Gross motor (climbing, etc.)	33	61
Painting/drawing	29	2
Puzzles	23	5
Music	22	10
Constructional (e.g. Lego)	18	11
Sand/water, play	15	12
Exploring	9	—
Play-doh, plasticene, etc.	4	—
Rough-and-tumble play	—	26
Table-top games with rules	—	7
Games with rules (hide and seek)	—	18
Watching others	—	6

activities of children under the age of five years. Although opinions differ as to the function of fantasy in the play of the young child (Sherrod and Singer, 1977; Smith and Syddall, 1978), many writers would agree with Newson and Newson (1968) in their description of its potential:

> The exercise of his imagination through the medium of fantasy allows the child to manipulate the whole spectrum of human feeling to accommodate to his own emotional needs; in particular, by playing at being someone else he comes to break the bonds of his own egocentricity, and to begin to comprehend and respect the needs and desires of other people. (p. 174)

With regard to children with Down's syndrome, Hill and McCune-Nicholich (1981) and Cunningham, Glenn, Wilkinson and Sloper (1985) conclude that symbolic ability as assessed through play is highly correlated with both cognitive ability and interpersonal development. In both studies it was noted that children with Down's syndrome passed through a similar developmental progression of play as that noted in non-handicapped children. In the cohort, representational object play, e.g. pushing a toy car along making 'brrm brrm' noises or singing a doll to sleep, was described by 48 per cent of mothers. More elaborate pretend play, e.g. where a plate is transformed in the child's imagination into a steering wheel, or where fantasy roles such as teacher or doctor, are adopted by the participants, was reported for 37 per cent of the children when they played alone and 48 per cent when they played with others:

> She plays with her dolls and teddies . . . copies me with the baby and has tea parties.

> She plays at school with her teddies, she's the teacher and she pretends she's an Avon lady.

Davie *et al.* (1984) describe few age differences in activities between their three-year-old and five-year-old samples. However, by the time non-handicapped children reach the age of seven years, their activities have changed considerably. Newson and Newson (1976b) describe a decrease in fantasy play, with a corresponding increase in drawing, reading and writing, model-making, sewing and knitting and games such as Monopoly and Ludo. Such activities were mentioned rarely by mothers in our study. Although there are few differences between the activities of the children with Down's syndrome and non-handicapped children of three to five years of age, the activities expected of non-handicapped children at seven years of age were not reported by the mothers we interviewed. Since the developmental level of the children in the cohort ranged between two and six years, their play closely approximates that expected for their developmental stage.

All of the mothers in the cohort said that their children enjoyed at least some activities. However, twelve per cent did say (some with anger and some with humorous exasperation), that their child's favourite activity was either eating or being destructive:

> Her favourite activity is wrecking the place, smashing the house up . . . spoiling the other children's games.

In response to a question asking 'For how long can you leave your child without supervision?', mothers' replies are shown in Table 3.6. This question relates to the child's ability to occupy him/herself, but also to the extent to which the occupation chosen is safe and useful. It is an important question, as it gives some indication of the amount of freedom and space that mothers can enjoy. Many mothers responded as would the mothers of all young children:

Table 3.6: Time the children can be left unsupervised

Time	% of children
Less than 15 minutes	9
15 – 30 minutes	41
30 minutes – 1 hour	28
More than 1 hour	20

Well, quite a while really, unless he's very quiet and that's when I know he's up to something.

This was significantly related to the child's age and to the number of behaviour problems shown by the child. Parents of older children and those whose children showed few behaviour problems were able to leave them alone for longer. This did not significantly vary with the child's health or social ability. Mothers who received the early intervention service felt able to leave their children alone for significantly longer than those mothers who did not receive the service. This may reflect increased parental confidence as a consequence of the early support they received.

Friends

Friendships are among the central ingredients of children's lives from as early as age 3 and, in some cases even earlier. Children's relationships with their peers directly affect their well-being, provide an opportunity to learn and practise social skills, and may establish enduring patterns of relating to others.

(Rubin and Sloman, 1984, p. 233)

For the purposes of this chapter, friends will be broadly defined as any children with whom the child played regularly. Such a broad definition is necessary because of the wide age range of the children in the sample. We describe home-based friendships first, i.e. friendships with neighbours, relatives and the children of mothers' friends. Then we move on to consider friendships with other children at school. This is because the younger children in the sample only had home-based friendships. Also, although for older children, home-based and school-based friendships may be interlinked, this is more difficult when a child attends a special school that caters for children with learning difficulties from a wide area and may be a considerable distance from home.

The nature of these home-based relationships varied considerably. In some cases, mothers described friends as adopting a 'caretaking' role, whereas in others, the relationships seemed more equal:

> They all look after him, play football, cowboys and Indians, police or just go round on their bikes.

> He plays their games, the kids recognize his limitations.

> Now he's gained his independence and he's always got his friends. It's — can he call for Stuart, or he just tells me he's going to call for who he's going to call for. So, off he goes and plays out. He mixes very, very well.

Some mothers recognised that although their children did not have friends, they were peripherally involved in the play of other children:

> I don't think she actually plays with them. She's just on the fringe. They're playing and as long as they're there, she's quite happy to do her own thing, but she's not actually playing with them as such.

Over 60 per cent of the children had at least one friend, mostly the children of neighbours. Other playmates included the children of the mother's friends, the children of relatives, and siblings' friends (see Table 3.7). Only eleven per cent of the children in the whole sample met other children through school. This largely reflects the fact that many of them travelled some distance to attend special schools. Where friends were the children of the mothers' friends or of relatives, families were, of necessity, involved in arranging for the children to meet so they could play together. This was often a much more formal arrangement than children meeting neighbours outside. Such arrangements could occupy a considerable amount of parents' time, particularly when children were younger and there were no other children living close by. This is also found in studies of the friendships of non-handicapped children (Rubin and Sloman, 1984).

Tables 3.7 and 3.8 describe the children's friends in terms of

Table 3.7: The children's friends

	% of children
Has friends, plays out often	13
Has friends, plays under supervision often	48
Has friends, sees rarely	5
Has no friends	34
Source of friends	**% of children**
Children of neighbours	58
Children of mother's friends	35
Relatives	22
Friends of siblings	17
Children at school	11
Other	8

Table 3.8: Number and ages of friends

Number of friends	**% of children**
None	34
One	18
Two–Four	23
Five or more	25
Age of friends	**% of children**
Older than child	20
Younger than child	26
Same age as child	12
Mixture of ages	43

frequency of contact, source of friends, number and age. There was no significant relationship between the age or the social age of the children and whether or not they had friends. There was also no relationship between the children's health and whether or not they had friends. Older children and children who were socially more mature were more likely to 'play out' with their friends. Also, children with health or medical problems were significantly less likely to 'play out' with their friends than were children with no problems. This could be related to difficulties experienced by the children. Those children with severe heart complaints may have found it difficult to keep up with other children. Children with poor eyesight or hearing may also have found it difficult to follow the activities of the group. Other children may have deliberately excluded such children, although no mothers referred to this. It is possible also that mothers of children with health or medical problems may have prevented their children from 'playing out' in order to protect them.

The proportion of children who were said by their mothers to play outside frequently is quite small (13 per cent). The reasons for not 'playing out' varied. Sixty-five per cent of mothers felt that their children were likely to wander or run off, if not supervised. In some cases, traffic hazard limited the freedom a child could be allowed. Whatever the reason, it was often noted as a source of frustration both to the children and their mothers:

> She'd like to be able to play out properly with other children, ride a bike. But if she's mobile, she's off. Someone has to be with her.

> If you let her out in the garden she disappears. You've got to watch her every minute.

> There are no facilities for playing out. The front door opens onto the street, and there's only a tiny yard at the back.

These reasons are also cited by Newson and Newson (1968) for restrictions in the play of their sample of non-handicapped four-year-olds.

The number of friends a child had increased with age. Thus, 34 per cent of the children under the age of five who had friends had only one friend, whereas for children of five to ten years, 19 per cent had only one friend. This corresponds to the findings of Lewis *et al.* (1984) who studied the social networks of young non-handicapped children. They found that six year olds were in regular contact with many more children than were three year olds.

The cohort children's friends were mostly a mixture of ages (43 per cent) or were younger than the child with Down's syndrome (26 per cent). One mother made the following observation about her child's playmates:

> Yes, she plays with quite a few children. It's funny really because as the little ones get a bit bigger, she plays with their younger brothers and sisters, you know what I mean. The other children kind of grow away and she plays with the next generation.

Another mother made the same observation, rather more succinctly:

The children grow out of him, you see.

This is likely to become more of a problem as the children grow older and the gap between them and their non-handicapped peers widens. Parents may find themselves retaining their involvement in their children's friendships by initiating and organising activities in order to enable friendships to continue.

Professionals need to be aware of the implications of this for educational integration. Both the activities and the friendships of the children in the cohort reflect their developmental level, rather than their chronological age. This suggests that we should not expect success if we insist on a rigid adherence to chronological age streaming in preschools and schools. A child with Down's syndrome may integrate much more successfully in the infant school if he/she starts at six years of age, rather than five. The same child may benefit much more from an extra year at nursery school or class.

Very few children played with other children with learning difficulties (16 per cent). The proportion of the sample who played with other children frequently (61 per cent) is higher than that given by Newson and Newson (1968) for four-year-old children in Nottingham (56 per cent), but is lower than that given for the same children at seven years of age (77 per cent) (Newson and Newson, 1976b).

Of the 42 children in the sample who had no friends, the greatest proportion of mothers said that it was because there were no young children around (14) or because the child was too young (14). Six said that other children were aware that the child was different or could not follow their games:

The children notice that he's different and don't really include him.

They all stand there staring at him . . . he comes in.

Only one child was teased by the local children, although three children had experienced teasing at preschool. Three mothers felt that their child's attendance at a special school prevented them from making friends with local children, who all attended the same school. One mother said that her child's poor health (a serious heart condition) prevented her from making friends and one, that her child's behaviour problems disrupted potential friendships.

The latter child damaged other children's toys and was inclined to hit or pinch other children.

We now move on to consider school-based friendships in more detail. As part of Study 2: Views about school, we asked mothers about their children's friendships at school. It is important to note that mothers may not know in detail about these friendships. School is an important source of social contacts for children, where they learn to develop their own peer-group relationships independently of their parents. In mainstream primary schools, which are normally near home, children can play with school friends after school. However, for those children in this sample who do not attend the neighbourhood school, and who may travel some distance to school, this does not happen so easily. Only ten children (17 per cent) played with school friends outside school and those in schools for children with severe learning difficulties (SLD) were least likely to do this.

Regardless of the type of school, even for those children who did have contact with school friends outside school, such contact was infrequent. Three children played at least once a week with school friends, and others less often. Only five children invited others home for tea or were invited by others. The main reason given for such lack of contact was that the other children lived too far away. A few parents mentioned lack of parental contacts that would enable them to arrange visits:

If I had more contacts with other parents at school through meetings and things, I would be able to invite children home and help his friendships.

Despite this, many children were said to have best friends at school. Thirty-five (58 per cent) currently had one or more best friends, four (seven per cent) had had one in the past, 13 (22 per cent) never had and eight (13 per cent) mothers did not know. This is somewhat smaller than the 76 per cent of seven-year-olds who had best friends in Newson and Newson's study (1976b).

Parents' views on friendships at school were varied. Twenty-nine (48 per cent) thought it very important for their children to have friends at school, and only four thought it was not important. Some parents emphasised the importance of different friends at home as opposed to school, especially when the child attended a special school:

Not so important at school, more at home. I would like her to

37

find normal children to play with at home because I think it would be more beneficial to her than playing with the same children all the time.

Others were aware of the difficulties their children may face in making friends, as illustrated in the following quote from a mother whose child was one of the ten per cent attending a mainstream setting:

In general, I think friends are quite important. I think they are less important for her. I think I have actually steeled myself to the fact that she probably isn't likely to have very many friends. You see, having chosen normal education for her, there aren't very many Mums who necessarily want her to be best friends with their child so I haven't encouraged that because I don't want to put anybody in a difficult position.

Study 4: Family relationships and the children's behaviour, also investigated the children's relationships with peers. Information on peer relationships is available for 44 children from both Study 3 and Study 4. For 33 (75 per cent), the rating had remained similar. There were no problems in peer relationships for 27 children, and continuing problems over the two-year gap for six children. For the remaining eleven children, relationships had improved in six cases, and deteriorated in five cases. There was no evidence therefore that relationships with peers deteriorated with increasing age (up to the age of ten). For most children, if they were sociable and mixed easily, this was not likely to change as they got older, within this age range of two to ten years.

Sisters and brothers

Brothers and sisters know us like no one else. They have been with us during the good times and the bad. Siblings constitute our first social network, and their early influence affects us throughout our lives. Our sibling relationships are typically the longest relationships we will have in our lives.

(Powell and Ogle, 1985)

Most of the children in the cohort at the time of Study 3 had at least one sibling (89 per cent). These ranged in age from a few months to 28 years. Nineteen per cent of the children had both older and younger siblings, 53 per cent had older siblings only and 18 per cent had younger siblings only. The vast majority played regularly with their siblings, both when the children were alone together (92 per cent) and when the siblings had friends home (83 per cent):

They all got on smashing.

I was really surprised, all the kids are great with him.

This is very similar to the figures given by Newson and Newson (1968; 1976b) for non-handicapped children of four years of age and seven years of age and by Carr (1975) for four-year-old children with Down's syndrome. The reason most frequently given by the mothers we interviewed for siblings not playing with the child with Down's syndrome was that the child could not understand the rules of the games and/or disrupted the games.

Not as many children went out to play with their siblings as played with them at home (60 per cent). The reason given by the majority of mothers where this did not occur was that the child needed more supervision than the sibling could provide. One-third of these mothers also said that it was unfair to expect the sibling to take on this extra responsibility. Only one mother said that the sibling was embarrassed.

In general, 72 per cent of mothers felt that the children got on well together. When Study 4: Family relationships and the children's behaviour, was carried out two years later, 83 per cent of the 60 cohort children aged between five and ten years who were included in this study had no problems in their relationships with siblings, 14 per cent had some problems and three per cent had marked problems. Marked problems were noted in those families where play between siblings was disrupted or prevented most of the time. One woman described a particularly difficult relationship between her six-year-old daughter Jean, and her older sister, Susan:

They rarely do anything together. Susan can't cope with Jean, she's in a separate world. They don't understand each other. Jean plays Susan up. She whinges. Susan gets ratty with her. I wish I could just turn off.

It is important to remember, however, that this is an exception and is only representative of three per cent of the families in the cohort.

Sibling relationships appear to be good in this group of children, and to be at least as good, if not better than in families of non-handicapped children. (This is discussed more fully in Chapter 4.) Also, relationships appear more likely to improve with time than to deteriorate. Forty-three families, in which there were siblings, participated in both Study 3 and Study 4. Over the two-year time period, the quality of sibling relationships remained the same in 30 families (good in 27 of these and poor in three). In ten families, relationships improved and relationships deteriorated in only three families.

It is possible that problems are relatively uncommon because siblings are encouraged by their parents to be helpful and understanding towards their brother or sister with Down's syndrome. In an interview study carried out by Miller (1974), siblings indicated that their parents did not tolerate them expressing negative feelings about the family member with learning difficulties. Hart and Walters (1979) found that siblings wanted to know how best to help their brother or sister.

Table 3.9 presents the problems mentioned by the (32) 28 per cent of women in Study 3 who felt that their children did not get on well together.

Table 3.9: Problems in sibling relationships

Problems	Frequency (32 children)
Child is aggressive	13
Siblings jealous	7
Child disturbs siblings at night	6
Child disrupts siblings' games	5
Child damages siblings' possessions	4

When asked directly whether or not the siblings ever felt left out, 42 per cent of the women in the whole sample thought that this happened:

> Jim was jealous when he was younger, he didn't understand. I got him involved in helping with Paul, and now he spends every minute with him.

> She gets a bit sulky and grumpy . . . then resentful. I keep her up a bit later and give her some extra time that way.

On the other hand, some families were particularly concerned that this should not happen:

> I hope they don't feel left out. I hope they all feel of value. We've been to great pains to make sure that they do. They're all children first and they're so different. We try to give each child what they need . . . We do get normal family rivalries.

Newson and Newson (1968) report figures of 33 per cent for jealousy in siblings of non-handicapped children. They express doubts about this figure, and feel it may be an underestimate (Newson and Newson, 1976b). They conclude that mothers were unwilling to admit jealousy in their children. This is less likely to have happened in our interview as we did not use the word 'jealous' but instead, asked if the children ever felt 'left out'. In a similar interview study to that of Newson and Newson (1968), Carr (1975) reported that almost half of the mothers she interviewed felt that the siblings were jealous of the child with Down's syndrome. The children with Down's syndrome in Carr's study were four years of age at the time. Jealousy and rivalry between siblings is common in many families at particular stages, whether there is a child with learning difficulties or not (Dunn and Kendrick, 1980; 1981) and appears to be no higher in families of children with learning difficulties (Newson and Newson, 1968).

We asked mothers in our study, how they were aware that the siblings felt 'left out'. Their replies are shown in Table 3.10. Because they described attention-seeking, regression, withdrawal and difficult behaviour, we wished to find out whether the presence of a child with Down's syndrome was associated with behaviour problems in siblings. In order to do this, as part of Study 4: Family relationships and the children's behaviour, we asked mothers to fill in questionnaires for each sibling.

Table 3.10: Siblings who felt 'left out'

How this was shown	Frequency (46 children)
Seeks reassurance	18
Tells mother	13
Demands attention	10
Withdraws	10
Difficult behaviour	10
Regression	8
Problems at school	4

Mothers completed either the Behaviour checklist (BCL) (Richman *et al.*, 1982) or the Rutter Scale A (Rutter *et al.*, 1970) depending on the age of the sibling. The proportions of children who scored over the cut-off points on these scales were comparable or even slightly smaller than in the standardisation samples, suggesting that siblings of children with Down's syndrome are not any more likely to develop problems than any other children. We also found that such problems were more likely to occur in families where there were general relationship problems within the family. This suggests that the problems were not a response to the child with Down's syndrome. They occurred in association with poor marital relationships, poor relationships between the mothers and their children with Down's syndrome and also high maternal Malaise Scores.

Gath (1973) reports similar findings on sibling behaviour problems in her study of young children with Down's syndrome (birth to two years), and in a follow-up study when the children were eight years old (Gath and Gumley, 1984). Carr and Hewett (1982) also conclude that the siblings of eleven-year-old children with Down's syndrome show similar, low levels of behaviour problems to the siblings of non-handicapped control children. Where there were behaviour problems in the siblings, Gath (1978) concluded that the children in question had problems before the birth of the child with Down's syndrome. In a larger-scale survey of the siblings of children with Down's syndrome, Gath (1973) found that older sisters of children with Down's syndrome were more often rated as antisocial by their teachers than were the sisters of non-handicapped children. However, those who were rated as antisocial were from larger families, with older mothers, from social classes IV and V. They were thus subject to many difficulties, and were not simply responding to the presence of a sibling with Down's syndrome.

A small proportion of the children in our sample (nine per cent) were teased by their siblings. Where this happened, mothers thought that it was not serious and reflected normal family interactions. To the mothers' knowledge, rather more of the siblings (24 per cent) had been teased by their friends or peers about their sibling with Down's syndrome. The majority of mothers were content to leave their children to deal with this when it happened. Eight had explained to the sibling why it happened, and only six had intervened.

The answers to all of the questions asked about sibling relationships combine to suggest that, if anything, these are better in the cohort families than in families of non-handicapped children. However, in order to state this conclusion firmly, one would need concurrent data on families of non-handicapped children in which the effects of social class, family size and maternal age were controlled for. This is not to suggest that sibling relationships are completely free of problems. Hart and Walters (1979) in their interview study of siblings, asked about their needs and views rather than about their interactions. The children they interviewed expressed a desire for more information about the disabilities, resources and methods of helping. They also needed guidance on child management and genetic counselling, and contact with other siblings. Similar needs have been identified by Powell and Ogle (1985).

Factors related to difficulties in activities and relationships

We now have a picture of how the children in the cohort spend their days. We know what sorts of things they do and how they get on with other children. We know that a relatively small proportion of them have difficulties — some cannot be left alone by their parents for more than a few minutes, some have no friends, some have few activities that they enjoy and some do not get on well with sisters and brothers. We need to identify who these children are, whether they have difficulties in more than one area and what factors are associated with the difficulties. Then we can begin to consider ways of meeting their needs.

In order to do this, we looked first at the children's activities and relationships with friends. For each child, we combined all of the information we had on this topic into one measure called 'child's friends and play'. A child with a low rating on this measure had no friends, could not be left alone to play for more than a few minutes, attended no clubs or classes and enjoyed few activities. A high rating indicated the opposite. We then examined the relationship between child, parent and family characteristics and the 'child's friends and play' rating, using analyses of variance (see Appendix, p. 155). The characteristics which we considered are listed in Table 3.11. The results of the analyses indicated that two of these characteristics were associated with the ratings on the measure 'child's friends and play':

Table 3.11: Child, parent and family characteristics

Child characteristics	Family characteristics
Age	Number of parents
Sex	Number of children
Family position	Social class
Placement i.e. fostered/adopted	Religion
Medical problems	House ownership
Social quotient	Health of siblings
Social age	Family sharing
Behaviour problems	Informal support
	Professional support
Parent characteristics	Support from religion
Age of parents	
Parental education	
Mother's employment	
Father's employment	

(1) Child's social age — children with a low social age likely to be restricted in their friends and activities.

(2) Behaviour problems — those children with many behaviour problems more likely to be restricted in their friends and activities.

We then combined all of the information we had on each child's relationships with sisters and brothers to form a measure that we called 'sibling relationships'. A high rating on this measure indicated that sisters and brothers played frequently with the child with Down's syndrome, included the child in their activities, had few quarrels with the child and did not tease or resent their sibling. Children who had good relationships with their siblings were not necessarily those who had few difficulties in their play and their relationships with friends. The two measures were slightly positively correlated with each other, but this was not significant.

We carried out a similar series of analyses to discover which of the two characteristics listed in Table 3.11 were related to sibling relationships. The results indicated that two of these factors were closely associated with sibling relationships:

(1) Family position — least problems in sibling relationships were likely to be found where the child with Down's syndrome was the oldest in the family, and most problems where he/she was either the youngest or in the middle.

(2) Behaviour problems — sibling relationships were most

likely to be difficult when the child with Down's syndrome had many difficulties in behaviour.

These two sets of findings are supported by similar analyses that we carried out as part of Study 4: Family relationships and the children's behaviour. Here too, we found that difficulties in relationships with peers were more likely in children with lower developmental scores, particularly IQ and verbal comprehension and with higher rates of behaviour problems.

It makes sense that autonomy in play and relationships comes with developmental maturity. It is also likely that in order to play with other children, a child needs to have some comprehension both of the games being played and of the conversation of peers. The association between difficulties in play and relationships and high rates of behaviour problems could be for two different reasons. Firstly, a child with behaviour problems such as running away frequently will be prevented from 'playing out' and possibly from attending clubs and classes by parents. Such a child will have few opportunities for autonomy in play. A second reason for the association with behaviour problems is the likelihood of other children rejecting a child who is seen as aggressive, difficult or unpredictable.

In Study 4, we found that difficult, attention-seeking children and those who are moody and irritable are likely to have problems in relationships within the family. This may also explain the association between behaviour problems and sibling-relationship problems. We do not know which of these factors causes the other. It is likely that each influences the other, with poor family relationships influencing child behaviour and difficult child behaviour also influencing family relationships.

As far as family position is concerned, in families where the child with Down's syndrome is the oldest and has always been there as far as younger siblings are concerned, it may be that there are less problems of adjustment and less resentment than in families where the child with Down's syndrome is a middle or youngest child. In their review of the literature on children with disabilities and their siblings, Simeonsson and Bailey (1986) similarly conclude that siblings who are older than the child with a disability may be more vulnerable, although the size of the gap in age between the siblings is also important and may alter this.

The findings from these two sets of analyses indicate that as far as the child's activities and relationships are concerned, these are strongly associated with the child's behaviour. This relationship is likely to be circular, with each factor influencing the other. Where there are behaviour problems, there are also likely to be difficult or poor relationships with sisters, brothers and with friends. Relationships within the family generally are likely to be difficult. The child's play and activities are thus adversely affected and restricted. In the next chapter, we describe the frequency and type of behaviour problems shown by the children in the cohort and the factors associated with these.

Summary

This chapter describes how the children in the cohort spend their days. The majority of those under the age of five attended a pre-school setting, and for over half of these, the setting was an integrated one. This is not the case for many other families of children with learning difficulties. One of the effects of our early intervention appeared to be that it enabled more mothers to seek out a placement in an ordinary preschool setting for their child. However, this effect was not found in the school setting. Of the children who were five years of age or older, 18 per cent attended integrated settings. The remainder travelled some distance from home to special schools, making it difficult for them to mix with local children. Over half of these school age children attended clubs or classes outside school.

The activities and friendships of the children in the cohort are very similar to those of non-handicapped children of three to five years of age. Watching television, gross motor activities, pretend play and looking at books were the most frequent activities. However, the children in the cohort differed considerably from seven-year-old, non-handicapped children, both in terms of their favourite activities and their friendships. The stages of their play and the activities they enjoyed reflected their developmental rather than their chronological age. Similarly, they interacted more in the neighbourhood with children of a similar developmental level. This has some implications for educational integration and suggests that we should not expect success if we insist on a rigid adherence to chronological-age streaming. Early separation at different and often distant schools means that children may be deprived of opportunities both to develop relationships with other children and to learn how to play and interact, using them as models.

Approximately one-third of the children had difficulties in that they could not be left to play alone and/or had no friends. These tended to be children who were developmentally and socially more severely handicapped and those with many behaviour problems. One expects that a child who is developing very slowly will have few friends and will need more adult intervention. However, if the child also exhibits very difficult behaviour, the difficulties in play and relationships are likely to be more severe, and perhaps require specific, specialist intervention.

Relationships with siblings were excellent in the majority of families and problems appeared to be less frequent than in families of non-handicapped children. Where there were difficulties, these were more likely to occur if the child with Down's syndrome was a middle or youngest child, suggesting that in such families parents and siblings need more help and advice than they currently receive. When the child with Down's syndrome had many behaviour problems, sibling relationships were also more likely to be difficult.

When behaviour problems occur, they point to major restrictions and difficulties in the lives of children with Down's syndrome. The next chapter describes these problems and the factors associated with them.

4

The Children and their Parents

In this chapter, we consider the children and their relationships with their parents. Three aspects of these relationships are described. First, we focus on parental management of behaviour. We consider the extent to which mothers feel that they treat the child with Down's syndrome differently to other children, and describe their attitudes about and practices of specific management techniques. Concerns about management were frequently raised by parents during informal discussions with members of the research team. Understandably, this was particularly the case where parents felt that their children were difficult to manage.

The second focus of this chapter is a description of difficulties in behaviour shown by the children. We examine both the frequency and severity of specific problems, and mothers' concerns and anxieties regarding these. The third focus is a broader considera-tion of the parent – child relationship. There are many more facets to this relationship than just that of management. We examine the rewards that mothers feel their children have brought them and their families. We discuss mothers' enjoyment of their children, and the warmth and affection with which they speak of them.

Having considered these three aspects of the parent – child relationship, the chapter concludes with an examination of the factors that appear to be associated with high levels of behaviour problems. In the previous chapter, we noted the important implications of this for children's activities and relationships both within the family and with peers. We hope that this will provide some guidelines for parents and for those who work with families to enable them to prevent or to reduce the occurrence of such difficulties.

Child management

For every man and woman, the control of children is a part of
real experience: for all of us, the basic stuff of our memories;
for some of us, an immediate practical issue in our relationship with our own growing families; for most of us, something
which we also watch and assess in other people.

(Newson and Newson, 1968, p. 412)

For mothers of children with learning difficulties, this issue may be
surrounded by uncertainty. Their children have special needs and
they may not be sure how to take these needs into account. In their
concern that their children should be socially integrated, they may
feel that the behaviour of the children should be more than just
acceptable. They may be even more aware than other parents that
their child, and thus their child management, is being watched and
assessed by others. One mother described the uncertainty as
follows:

It's like acting in a play without knowing the words, or adding
up a sum and not knowing if it's the right answer. Your child is
different and you're not sure how to deal with him.

In both Study 3 and Study 4, we asked mothers how they felt
about management in general. In both cases, almost half were
unhappy with some aspects, or found their children difficult to
manage at times (Table 4.1). Newson and Newson (1968) found

Table 4.1: Feelings about management

	% of mothers	
	Study 3	Study 4
No problems	54	55
Some concerns/difficulties	42	36
Many concerns/difficulties	4	9

that a similar, or even larger, proportion of mothers of non-handicapped children (54 per cent) expressed similar worries. For the
majority, these concerns do not appear to pass with time. Seventy-
five per cent of those mothers who took part in both studies and
who were expressing concern at the time of Study 3 were still
concerned at the time of Study 4, two to three years later. For the

remainder, (25 per cent) there had been some improvement. Of those cohort mothers who were concerned, 40 per cent felt that they sometimes overreacted or were impatient, and 26 per cent felt that they were not strict enough:

> I feel a bit guilty about this. I think I should be more firm with him.

> I think half of it is my handling of him, and his way of growing up, and because he's the youngest he's been the spoilt one.

The majority of mothers approved of smacking in principle, only ten per cent expressed disapproval. A similar proportion rarely or never smacked their children. This is similar to the findings of Newson and Newson (1968) for non-handicapped children. The proportions of mothers using different types of management techniques are shown in Table 4.2. After physical punishment,

Table 4.2: Management techniques

	% of mothers
Physical punishment	91
Time out	51
Verbal punishment	47
Threats	27
Withdrawal of privileges	26

i.e. smacking, the most frequent management technique used was 'time out', which meant sending the child to a 'naughty corner', a 'naughty chair' or to his/her room for a short period. Most parents used a combination of techniques, depending on the behaviour and the situation. The range of techniques used by different mothers is expressed by the following quotes:

> We usually, sounds awful this doesn't it, put her in the naughty corner. Now, our naughty corner is in the kitchen where the two worktops meet and we just say 'Go and stand in the naughty corner' and she'll go just for a couple of minutes, that's sufficient for her.

> We smack him, or stop him playing out, or take his privileges off him.

Smack. Raised voice. Totally against educational psychology, but there you go. They're not altogether backing up smacks, are they? But it works. I think for children like this you need a very quick 'yes' or 'no', 'should' or 'shouldn't', and that's one hell of a way of letting them know.

I've never been one for physical punishment, so he's never been hit. The biggest punishment for him is to be withdrawn from activities and to have our disapproval, actually. He's very easy to punish. He gets very upset if he knows you disapprove.

The majority of mothers also rewarded their children for 'good' behaviour, the most frequent rewards being praise, a clap or a hug. Just over half of the mothers we interviewed felt that they treated the child with Down's syndrome differently to their other children (53 per cent). Most of these felt that they were less strict with the child with Down's syndrome (46 per cent), with only eight per cent being more strict. Forty-seven per cent felt that there were no differences in the way they treated their children:

He's told off or smacked if he's naughty, just like the others.

We asked mothers if management difficulties ever made them feel like slamming the door and walking out. Eighteen per cent of the cohort had actually done this, 48 per cent said they sometimes felt like it and 33 per cent never felt like it. In contrast, 70 per cent felt that they never became so angry or frustrated with their children that they feared losing control. Twenty per cent said that it sometimes happened, and ten per cent that they frequently feared losing control, and occasionally did. Those who feared losing control were not necessarily the same as those who expressed concerns about management. This was another of the instances where mothers in the cohort, who had received early intervention from the research team, differed from those who had not received early intervention. More of the cohort mothers feared losing control. It may be that one of the effects of the open relationship with the research team and the early support they received was to make it easier for them to acknowledge and express such fears:

Yes, I think we want it (i.e. help or advice) because sometimes it can get to the stage where you want to put your hands round her neck, quite honestly.

Behaviour difficulties

There are two stereotypes held about people with Down's syndrome. The first is that they are 'affectionate, placid and docile', and the second that they are 'sullen and stubborn' (Smith and Berg, 1976). These clearly conflict and, like the descriptive labels that are attached to any distinct group, for example, women or black people, can lead to discrimination, hostility and oppression (Barton, 1986; Booth, 1985). It is likely that these labels can be applied to some children with Down's syndrome at some times, as they could be applied to many children. They do not help either parents or service providers, however. Given that 30 per cent of mothers feared losing control with their children at least sometimes, and that 45 per cent had concerns about management, it is important to describe the types of difficulties in behaviour that the children showed, the frequency and severity of these difficulties and the factors associated with them.

As part of Study 3: The child, the family and the community, mothers were asked what it was about their children that they found hardest to cope with. As Table 4.3 shows, the largest group

Table 4.3: What mothers found hardest to cope with

	% of mothers
Behaviour problem(s)	44
Developmental delay	18
Language/speech problem	9
Thinking about the future	5
Physical/health problem	4
Attitudes of others	4
Nothing difficult	16

found behaviour problems in their children hardest to deal with (44 per cent). Many cited such problems repeatedly throughout the interview as the reasons for difficulties and restrictions experienced by the child and the family, in their relationships and in their social and leisure activities. The same behaviours were not seen as problems by all families, however. Some families repeated that they had no more problems with the child with Down's syndrome than with their other children. Study 4: Family relationships and the children's behaviour, was carried out in order to explore these issues further.

Mothers were first asked whether they felt that anything in the behaviour of their child was a problem at the time of Study 4. Seventy-two per cent reported a definite problem, six per cent were not sure and 22 per cent were certain there was no problem. Then, they were asked a series of detailed questions about specific behaviours. These questions form the Behaviour Screening Questionnaire (BSQ), devised and used by Richman *et al.* (1982) with mothers of non-handicapped children aged three, four and eight-years-old. A second, shorter series of questions was also included. This was added because Gath and Gumley (1984) noted that scales devised for use with non-handicapped children did not cover many of the behaviours that parents of children with Down's syndrome were most concerned about. This second series of questions was derived from the work of Gath and Gumley (1984), Wing and Gould (1978), and from the behaviour difficulties described by cohort mothers during Study 3: The child, the family and the community.

No child scored zero on these two series of questions. As 22 per cent of mothers reported that there was nothing in their child's behaviour that was a problem, this indicated a difference between mothers' perceptions of a problem and the behavioural listings. This would suggest that a woman's perception of what constitutes a behaviour problem in her child is strongly influenced by factors other than the child's behaviour. Many women appeared to be aware of a problem, but were confident that they could cope with it and did not find it particularly distressing or disruptive. Some women had learned to live with, and adjust their lives to quite major difficulties. For example, the woman quoted below, when asked if her child slept through the night, replied:

No. No, she doesn't. Here's me saying I've got no problems! You take them for granted though, don't you, when you've had them for years, you know.

This indicates the importance of not simply asking parents if there are any problems and accepting their replies at face value. Parents should be given time to think about how things really are and should be asked specific questions in order to help them do this. The aim is not to discover a problem come what may, but to obtain a valid picture. If this is not done, parents may be left to cope with longstanding problems that could be relieved.

Table 4.4 shows the percentages of children for whom each of

Table 4.4: Percentage of children showing marked difficulties in behaviour: children with Down's syndrome (Study 4) compared to non-handicapped children of 3, 4 and 8 years of age (Richman et al., *1982)*

Behaviour	Study 4	Richman *et al.* (1982)			
		3	4	8	(years)
	%	%	%	%	
Poor appetite	1	19	20	13	
Faddy eating	3	15	14	15	
Soiling	8	16	13	4	
Night-wetting	18	34	19	4	
Day-wetting	23	26	8	2	
Difficulty settling in bed	20	16	15	12	
Sleeping in parents' bed	24	10	6	5	
Waking at night	41	14	12	3	
Dependency	0	6	5	8	
Overactive/restless	1	17	13	11	
Tantrums	4	5	6	9	
Miserable/irritable	2	4	7	7	
Sibling relationships	2	13	19	19	
Poor concentration	13	9	6	7	
Worries	2	4	10	21	
Attention-seeking	20	10	9	7	
Peer relationships	4	4	6	8	
Difficult to control	9	11	10	10	
Fears	15	10	12	2	

the items of behaviour in the BSQ was definitely present and was a marked problem. The most common behaviours were waking at night, sleeping in the parents' bed, difficulty settling at night, day and night-wetting, attention-seeking, poor concentration and fears. In the second series of questions about behaviours not included in the BSQ, the following problems were exhibited by at least 20 per cent of children: interfering with others' belongings, throwing objects, running away and behaving inappropriately to strangers. Embarrassing behaviour, such as taking their clothes off, aggressiveness, shouting and screaming, spitting and such habits as thumb- or finger-sucking, nail-biting and twiddling objects, were less frequent, but were still problems for more than ten per cent of the children. Mothers' descriptions of some of these behaviours and their impact on the family will give a clearer picture of the difficulties. When reading these, it is important to remember that the children described ranged between five and ten years of age.

She wakes up and either comes into our room or she shouts and quite often she decides she wants a drink and then I just take her her back to bed and if I just get in with her she goes off to sleep. Sometimes, she's awake and wants to play. She never goes through the whole night. Well, she has done occasionally and we sort of cheer in the morning when we wake up and realise she's slept through, but she usually wakes up once or twice.

One problem I have is trying to keep him in his bed all night, because at four o'clock in the morning he gets out of bed. He picks his small pillow up out of his bed and he goes into his sister's room, and he curls up in her bed with her. He can't stop with her for ever. Like she says, sometimes she's that tired, she just doesn't hear him come into bed, or feel him come into bed, until she wakens up the next morning.

She'll go up to strangers and try to kiss them. It's something we try to stop but it's very difficult, because people, they encourage her. They encourage her, and you know, they try and make you feel awful for trying to stop her. But if you don't stop it at this age, they're not going to like it when she's another two or three years older, and she's still doing it.

Only his saying 'hello' to people. I'm always trying to tell him, you know, you don't say 'hello' to everybody. Somebody will take you off one of these days. Good luck to them, but that's beside the point, you know.

Every morning in her bedroom, she throws everything around. She seems to do the same thing every morning. Any toys on her bed, the whole lot of come off. All the bedding comes off in the morning. Anything on the shelves. Every morning the same. No matter what you put in the room, everything comes off.

He runs away three or four times a week. The only thing is that I won't run after him. I stand there and I say, 'Right, you either come back now, or when you come back, I'll smack you.' . . . You see, the others tend to run after him, and I say, don't run after him. He's got to be made to come back. But he does do it quite a lot.

When he's either not got somebody's attention, or you leave

him on his own for too long, or he's generally upset about things, then he'll hurl things around the room.

She runs off as soon as your back is turned, straight into danger. You can't take your eyes off her. We have to keep all the doors and windows locked, and we can't leave anyone to mind her when she's awake. It prevents her playing with other children.

Oh, he runs away. He knows where he's going you see, he's a monkey. He wasn't lost according to him, because he knew where he was.

Oh yes, she'll hang around waiting for attention. She gets very, very insistent as well. You spend five minutes with her and then you get five minutes, and then she's back.

While we compare the behaviour difficulties described by the mothers of children with Down's syndrome with those described by the mothers of non-handicapped children (Table 4.4), it is important to bear in mind certain other differences between the two samples. The sample of families included in the study described by Richman *et al.* (1982) included more small families, fewer families who owned their own homes, fewer employed mothers and fewer fathers with further education. Also, the children with Down's syndrome had experienced many more stays in hospital. Many of these factors are associated with differences in rates of behaviour problems. Therefore, caution must be used when comparing the two groups.

The two groups of children also differ in chronological age. The average developmental age of the children with Down's syndrome was 39 months (ranging from six to 82 months), as calculated from the developmental assessments. This can be compared to Richman's three-year-olds. However, the impact on the family of some behaviour problems in a three-year-old cannot be considered as equivalent to the impact of the same problems in an older child.

Richman *et al.* (1982) state that a score of ten or above on the BSQ indicates major behaviour difficulties. This was supported by independent clinical ratings. They found that 14 per cent of the three-year-old children in their sample scored on or above the cut-off point: 17 per cent from manual and ten from non-manual social-class groups. In our sample of children with Down's syndrome, twelve per cent scored above the cut-off point: 17 per cent from manual and five from non-manual social-class groups. Thus, there does not appear to be any marked difference in the prevalence of major behaviour difficulties between groups at this developmental stage. This is in marked contrast to a study of a representative group of children with severe learning difficulties aged up to 16 years (Quine, 1986). Forty-five per cent of these children had severe or mild behaviour problems and the frequencies of destructive behaviours and self-injury was much higher. Prevalence did not vary with age in this sample.

Although the overall rate of major behaviour difficulties does not differ between the children with Down's syndrome and the group of non-handicapped children, it is clear from Table 4.4, that the types of problems do differ. Problems shown by a significantly higher proportion of the children with Down's syndrome are: sleeping problems, including settling at night, waking at night and sleeping with parents, poor concentration, attention-seeking and fears. Problems shown by a significantly higher proportion of non-handicapped children are: poor appetite, 'faddy' eating, over-activity, dependency, difficult relationships with siblings and recent-onset night-wetting.

Sleeping problems remain consistently high as the age of the children with Down's syndrome increases, whereas these reduce significantly with age for the non-handicapped children. An increase in the prevalence of sleeping problems has been found in other samples of children with learning difficulties (e.g. Carr, 1975; Clements, Wing and Dunn, 1986; Quine, 1986). It would appear that factors other than age or developmental status, such as parental management style may influence sleep problems.

In the non-handicapped group of children, the incidence of the 'worries' category increases from four to 21 per cent between three and eight years of age, whilst the 'fears' category reduces from ten to two per cent. Only two per cent of the children with Down's syndrome were rated as 'worriers', whereas 15 per cent were rated as having many fears. The 'worry' category refers to anxiety over imagined or anticipated events, whereas the 'fears' category refers to anxiety over actual and present events or situations. The difference between the two groups of children may reflect less ability to anticipate fearful events on the part of the children with Down's syndrome, due to differences in cognitive/developmental level.

The children with Down's syndrome were also more likely to have poor concentration and to be attention-seeking. These differences may again be related to cognitive factors, and may reflect less ability on the part of the children with Down's syndrome to initiate and organise their own activity, and attend to this for a reasonable period of time. Although attention-seeking is higher among the children with Down's syndrome, dependency is lower. This indicated that the non-handicapped children in Richman *et al.*'s (1982) study were more unwilling to be separated from mother and left with strangers. They were also more likely to have miserable or irritable moods and to be restless. These differences could mean that children with Down's syndrome are less emotional or less temperamental than non-handicapped children, as a number of reports suggest (Gibbs, 1984; Gibson, 1978; Sorce and Emde, 1982). Alternatively, the differences could also be due to children with Down's syndrome having less ability to anticipate fearful or distressing events, as discussed above.

The final, significant difference between the two groups is that the non-handicapped children showed a higher incidence of problems with siblings. Again, this could be due to the children with Down's syndrome being less emotional or temperamental and thus less likely to have arguments or rows with their siblings. It is puzzling, however, that relationship difficulties with peers are not similarly reduced in the group of children with Down's syndrome. This may be because some of the children in the cohort have few friends and their interactions with them are limited. It would seem likely that problems with siblings are also less common because the siblings are encouraged by their parents to be helpful and understanding towards their brother or sister with Down's syndrome (see Chapter 3). The lower incidence of difficulties in sibling relationships may be due to siblings' tolerance and desire to help.

It is important to remember that behaviours such as interfering with others' belongings, throwing objects, running away and behaving inappropriately to strangers were not included in the BSQ. These were problems for more than 20 per cent of the children with Down's syndrome. We cannot compare these frequencies to samples of non-handicapped children. There are likely to be greater problems of management and greater strain on the families where these problems occur.

Mother – child relationships

As well as asking the women who took part in Study 3: The child,

Table 4.5: What pleases mothers most about their children

	% of mothers
Happy, loving nature	35
Any new achievements	16
Everything	16
Doing better than family hoped	14
Sense of humour	5
Language skills	3
Other specific achievements	3
Doing well at school	2
Accepted by peers	2
Other	2
Can't think of anything	2

the family and the community, what they found hardest to cope with, we also asked what pleased them most about their children. Their replies are shown in Table 4.5. For 16 per cent of women, everything about their child pleased them. Despite concerns about behaviour difficulties and the anger and frustration that these often caused, only two per cent were not able to think of anything that pleased them at the time. Again, mothers' own words express these feelings eloquently:

I think she's really funny. She makes you laugh. It's funny. I'm very reserved. I'm not a toucher and yet with her it doesn't bother me, but sometimes it does with the others. Like if they fling their arms around my neck, I feel as though I've been over-powered, but she doesn't have that effect on me. It's queer . . . the irritation's not the same with her. Whether I excuse her or not, I don't know, but she doesn't irritate like if the others had done it . . . She hates it when I shout at her. It really upsets her. Then she'll say, 'Come and give me a love, come and give me a love, I'm sorry', and so you have to give her a cuddle then, you know, so that everything's all right . . . She's great really.

I just like him being there really, 'cos I know when he goes to my Mum's it's very quiet. I'm glad for the peace sometimes, but I find it very quiet.

He just comes up and sits on my knee and gives me a big kiss on the cheek and then he squeezes you round the neck. Even when we're out shopping, he does.

That he is playing with others, not just standing on the sidelines. He's more adaptable now and plays on his own more as well.

Her consideration for others. She puts her arm round them if they're upset.

She teaches her little sister. It's lovely that she can and wants to.

Just that she is my daughter.

He's coming on better than we ever imagined he would.

During Study 4, we wanted to find some way to rate or measure the mother–child relationship. We did this by noting the warmth and affection with which mothers spoke about their children, the positive or negative remarks they made about them, the acceptance they showed towards their children's personality or needs and the irritability or anger they showed towards them. The rating was made both on replies to direct questions on these topics and on any other comments made during the interviews. We noted facial expression, tone of voice and other aspects of non-verbal behaviour as well as what was actually said. This rating was derived from the work of Richman *et al.* (1982) and has been used to rate marital relationships also (e.g. Quinton, Rutter and Rowlands, 1976). During Study 4, two different researchers rated twenty mother–child relationships in order to check the reliability of this method. Percentage agreement between raters was 93 per cent.

Seventy-nine per cent of the relationships between the mothers and their children who participated in Study 4 were rated as 'good'. Eighteen per cent were rated as 'average', and three per cent were rated as 'poor'. No ratings of 'very poor' were made.

A rating of 'good' was made when the mother spoke of her child with marked warmth, concern and affection, when she and her child enjoyed each other's company and when she accepted her child's personality and needs. A rating of 'average' indicated less-marked warmth with some tensions. A rating of 'poor' was made when there was frequent irritation and many critical remarks, with lack of warmth and concern.

As one way of checking the validity of this rating, we asked mothers to complete a questionnaire called the Judson Self-Rating Scale (Judson and Burden, 1980). This scale gives some indication of mothers' attitude to their children and adjustment to the disability. Mothers' scores on this scale were found to be significantly positively correlated with the rating made by the interviewer of the mother–child relationship.

The small group of mothers who described severe management difficulties were more likely to have poor relationships with their children and to express little affection towards them. They were more likely to have low scores on the Judson Self-Rating Scale. They were also more likely to have high scores on the Malaise Inventory, indicating high levels of strain. This was the case regardless of the number of behaviour problems shown by the child.

Despite the concerns expressed by many women about their children's behaviour and about their own child-management techniques, the majority of mother–child relationships were characterised by their warmth, affection, enjoyment of each other's company and by the mother's recognition of the child's personality and needs. In the next section, we examine the impact of the mother–child relationship and of other characteristics of the children and their families on the occurrence of behaviour problems.

Factors influencing behaviour problems

We examined the relationship between child and family characteristics and the occurrence of behaviour problems using analyses of variance (see Appendix p. 151). The results indicate that the main factors associated with high BSQ scores and thus high levels of behaviour problems were:

(1) Employment status — children whose fathers were unemployed were more likely to show behaviour problems.
(2) Mothers' relationship with child — there tended to be more behaviour problems where the mother–child relationship was rated as poor.
(3) Mother's adjustment and attitude to the child (Judson self-rating scale) — there tended to be more behaviour problems where maternal adjustment was rated as low.
(4) The developmental status of the child — children with low developmental scores were more likely to show behaviour problems.

The same analysis was carried out including only those families where the fathers were employed. The results showed that the same factors were related to high levels of behaviour problems. In this case, the mother's stress level (as measured by the Malaise Inventory) became significant, with higher levels of behaviour problems where maternal stress was higher. Unlike previous suggestions in this area (Gibson, 1978), we found that behaviour problems did not vary significantly according to either the age or gender of the child.

These findings give a strong impression of similarity to non-handicapped children. As in our study, Richman *et al.* (1982) found that the ability of non-handicapped children, their relationships with their mothers and their mothers' attitudes to them were all related to behaviour problems. They also found that behaviour problems were higher in children who lived in council housing, particularly those living in high-rise flats. None of the families in the cohort lived in such accommodation. However, the link between paternal unemployment, maternal stress and behaviour problems in children with Down's syndrome appears to be similar. Richman *et al.* (1982) found a link between the parents' marital relationship and behaviour problems. However, in our study, marital difficulties did not have any impact on behaviour problems, provided the relationship between the mother and child remained strong. Thus, provided the parental subsystem is strong, discord in the marital subsystem does not appear to influence behaviour problems in the child.

Richman *et al.* (1982) report a high level of persistence of behaviour problems. They found that 61 per cent of problematic three-year-olds still showed significant difficulties five years later. Children were not growing out of their problems. Twenty-three children with Down's syndrome who were showing moderate or severe behaviour problems at the time of Study 3, were involved in Study 4 two to three years later. Seventeen of these children were still showing moderate or severe behaviour problems. This suggests that problems are just as persistent for children with Down's syndrome. Early help should be provided for families and the efforts of services providers should be concentrated on prevention. The factors listed earlier provide some indicators of which families may be at risk for the development of such problems.

Summary

This chapter describes the children's relationships with their parents. Almost half of the women we interviewed had lasting concerns about the way they handled their children and 30 per cent feared losing control at least sometimes. Most mothers used similar management strategies with the child with Down's syndrome as with their other children, although they were aware of the need to take the differences into account. For 44 per cent of mothers, it was behaviour problems that they found hardest of all to cope with.

Twelve per cent of the children with Down's syndrome described here showed serious behaviour difficulties as rated on the BSQ. There was no marked difference in the prevalence of such serious difficulties between these children and the sample of non-handicapped children of three, four and eight years of age studied by Richman *et al.* (1982).

However, the types of problems did differ considerably. The children with Down's syndrome were more likely to show sleeping problems, poor concentration, attention-seeking and fears. The non-handicapped children were more likely to show eating problems, overactivity, dependency, difficulties with sibling relationships and recent-onset night-wetting. Possible reasons for these differences include differences in management style, cognitive/developmental level and temperament. Problems not included in the BSQ and shown by more than 20 per cent of the children with Down's syndrome included interfering with others' belongings, throwing objects, running away and inappropriate behaviour to strangers.

Despite concerns about their children's behaviour, almost all of the mothers took great pride and pleasure in their children. Only two per cent could think of nothing that pleased them about the child. Seventy-nine per cent of the relationships between mothers and their children were characterised by their warmth, affection, enjoyment of each other's company and by the mothers' recognition of their children's personality and needs. In the minority of instances, where the mother–child relationship was rated as 'poor', these mothers were likely to describe their child as being difficult to manage and were experiencing high levels of stress. Some appeared to have difficulty in adjusting to the child's disability.

The children who exhibited serious behaviour difficulties were more likely to have low developmental scores. They were more likely to come from families where the father was unemployed and where their mother's adjustment to them was low, her relationship with them was poor and she experienced high levels of stress. Many of these factors are also associated with high levels of behaviour difficulties in non-handicapped children. These problems are likely to persist.

It is important to remember that a problem in a three- or four-year-old does not have the same impact as the same problem in an eight-year-old, especially if it has lasted for many years. There appears to be a large group of families who have one or two problems such as sleeping difficulties, but where the mother – child relationship is warm and strong, such problems should be amenable to direct intervention focused on child-management techniques. They could possibly be prevented by well-timed advice. There also appears to be a small group of families who had difficulties adjusting to the child and where the parent – child relationship is poor. This clearly requires a very different intervention, which is family focused and begins soon after the birth of the child. Service providers require a framework and a set of skills and materials to identify such families and offer the help they need (Cunningham and Davis, 1985b).

5

The Families:
Activities and Relationships

As applied to families, behavior and needs of individual
family members cannot be accurately and fully understood by
focusing on individual members in isolation . . . There are
properties of the family that can be understood only by studying the relationships among members and interactions among
its different dimensions.

(Turnbull *et al.*, 1986, p. 46)

Until now, we have focused on the children with Down's syndrome and their activities and relationships with sisters, brothers,
parents and peers. In this chapter, we broaden the focus and consider the activities of the family and other relationships within the
family unit.

First, we consider some of the activities and tasks that a family
needs to accomplish and describe how the families in the cohort
carry these out. We separate family activities into two quite distinct
areas: the first is that of housework and child care, whilst the second
concerns how the family meets the leisure, recreational and social
needs of its members. Following this, we explore the parents'
marital relationships. This is done in three ways: by considering the
process of decision-making with regard to the child with Down's
syndrome, by describing ratings we made of the quality and
strength of the relationships and by presenting mothers' views of
how their relationships with their husbands have changed.

Finally, we consider some of the ways in which the women in the
cohort feel that they themselves have changed as a result of having
a child with Down's syndrome. We describe maternal satisfaction
and stress and the factors that influence these.

Family activities: housework and child-care

In families with young children, housework and child-care tasks can be particularly time-consuming. Child-care tasks take longer when children need to be fed, washed, dressed, changed and supervised. Household tasks take longer when children cannot be left and cannot help. Many of the activities involved are repetitive and monotonous. Oakley (1974) compared ratings of household tasks with factory and assembly-line tasks and found that household tasks were described as more monotonous, fragmented and subject to time pressure. Because of this, the time and energy left over for leisure, recreation and socialisation is reduced in families with young children. There tends to be a drop-off in activities outside the home, and what leisure activity there is, takes place at home (Rapoport *et al.*, 1977). As parents have needs that are distinct from those of their children and may not be completely fulfilled simply by meeting their children's needs, this phase in the family lifecycle can be one of great tension.

In families where there is a child with learning difficulties, the child's needs for care and supervision may be greater than in families with non-handicapped children only. Household tasks may take longer and be more demanding. Also, as children with learning difficulties are dependent for longer, this phase may last longer and parents' enjoyment of progress towards independence may be reduced (Ayer and Alaszewski, 1984; Lonsdale, 1978; Wilkin, 1979).

We began to explore this topic by identifying 32 separate child-care and household tasks and asking mothers who did each of these and who helped. Two levels of help were defined: to *share* a task was to do half or more of the work, or to perform the task at least half the required number of times; to *help with* a task was to do less than half the work or to perform the task on fewer than half the required number of times. Table 5.1 presents the proportion of mothers in the cohort who performed tasks alone, who shared tasks, who received help with tasks or who were not involved in tasks because somebody else did them. The figures given are percentages. Where a task was not applicable to a family, for example, if the children washed or dressed themselves, then that family was excluded from the total. This table indicates that:

(1) Mothers were involved at some level in most tasks and performed a large proportion of them without any help.

Table 5.1: *Help received by mothers*

Child-related tasks	Mother alone %	Mother helped %	Mother shared %	Mother not involved %
Physical care of child e.g. dressing	24.5	44	25	6.5
Physical care of siblings	36	37	24	2
Playing with child	14	36	36	14
Playing with siblings	14	34	38	15
Hospital/doctor/school visits — child	66	13	20	1
Hospital/doctor/school visits — siblings	69	10	20	2

Household tasks	Mother alone %	Mother helped %	Mother shared %	Mother not involved %
Cooking/cleaning	66	24	7	3
Shopping	39	27	32	2
Washing dishes	20	36	23	21
Decorating/repairs	10.5	3.5	18	68

(2) They were helped more with child-related than with household tasks.

(3) For child-related tasks, more help was given with playing with the children than with their physical care. Least help was given with visits to the doctor, hospital or school.

(4) More help was given with the physical care of the child with Down's syndrome, than his/her siblings.

(5) The majority of mothers received little help with most household tasks, with the exception of washing dishes and shopping. The only tasks where mothers were minimally involved were decorating and household repairs.

These levels of helping and sharing are slightly higher than those described by Carey (1982) and Wilkin (1979), for mothers of children with severe learning difficulties.

Table 5.2 indicates where the help came from for each task. It describes the extent to which fathers, siblings and others either shared a task or assumed the major responsibility for it. The figures given are the percentage of families in the cohort for whom the task is applicable. This table indicates that:

Table 5.2: Who shares child-related and household tasks

Child-related tasks	Fathers %	Siblings %	Others %
Physical care of child e.g. feeding	25.5	3	1
Physical care of siblings	26	1	0.5
Playing with child	32	19.5	2
Playing with siblings	34	8.5	2
Hospital/doctor/school visits — child	21	0	1.5
Hospital/doctor/school visits — siblings	20	0	1.5

Household tasks	Fathers %	Siblings %	Others %
Cooking/cleaning	7	1	2
Shopping	31	2	1
Washing dishes	31	14	2
Decorating/repairs	79	0.5	6.5

(1) Fathers helped much more than any other family member or anyone outside the home. However, as shown in Table 5.1, this help was not extensive and the only tasks in which more than 30 per cent of fathers shared were, playing with the children, shopping, washing dishes and decorating or doing household repairs.

(2) The support available from siblings was much smaller, although it is important to remember that this was a sample of young children, and at least one-third of the families did not include children who were old enough to give support.

(3) The support available from outside the home was negligible.

This picture replicates that of Wilkin (1979) who used a similar detailed questionnaire with mothers to document exactly how much help of different types was received from various sources. The extent of help that mothers in the cohort received with child-care and household tasks does not differ markedly either from survey findings for other families who have children with learning difficulties (e.g. Ayer and Alaszewski, 1984; Carey, 1982) or from survey findings for families of non-handicapped children (Osborn *et al.*, 1984; Oakley, 1974).

Pahl and Quine (1984) found that fathers who were not working were more likely to help than employed fathers. In the cohort families, however, we found no significant differences between the families according to the employment status of the fathers. Also, the help received by mothers did not vary according to the extent or difficulty of the tasks. There were no significant differences according to social class, whether the mother was working outside the home, the health of the children, or the social ability of the child with Down's syndrome.

Given the low level of participation by anyone other than the mother in these tasks, we asked mothers about their satisfaction with the situation — whether they would like more help in the home and if they would like more time for themselves. Half of the women we interviewed said they would like more help (49 per cent). Of these, 19 per cent said they would like more help from the family and 30 per cent felt that this help should come from some service provision. Equal proportions said that they would like more help with housework, with teaching the child with Down's syndrome, or with child-minding. Similarly, 47 per cent of mothers said they would like more time for themselves, although one-third of these said that it was not the child with Down's syndrome who prevented them having time for themselves, but their situation as mothers of young children:

I can't even have a bath without the kids coming in.

I get as much time to myself as most women get.

This section indicates that the mothers we interviewed carried the main burden of household and child-care tasks, with little help from other family members or from anyone outside the family. This pattern is found in all families whether there is a child with learning difficulties or not, and whether the mother or the father are employed outside the home or not. As Graham (1984) concludes, 'Whatever the employment position of the family, it thus appears that it is typically the mother who looks after the house and looks after the children' (p. 61).

Family activities: leisure and recreation

In this section we examine the frequency with which parents went out together without the children, the frequency of family outings and of holidays. We explore the extent to which mothers felt that these activities were restricted by the child with Down's syndrome.

Parental outings

The frequency with which parents went out together without their children is given in Table 5.3. It is important to note that for 25 per cent of the families in the cohort, parental outings were very infrequent (i.e. less than 4 times per year). The frequency of parental outings did not vary with social class, the age of the child

Table 5.3: Frequency of parental outings (without the children)

	% of families
Weekly or more	36
Monthly or more	24
Every 2/3 months	15
Less or never	25

or with the child's social ability, or the level of behaviour problems. However, parents of children with severe health or medical problems were significantly less likely to go out together frequently:

> She probably stops us going out more than the other children. She doesn't sleep well and is often ill. We have to watch her very carefully because of her heart, so we tend to go out separately usually.

We asked mothers if they would like to go out more than they did. The majority (62 per cent) were content with the frequency of their outings:

> There's no problem. If we want to go out, we go out.

> My life centres around the home really.

Of the 38 per cent who said they would like to go out more often, only 15 per cent felt that the child with Down's syndrome prevented this and 23 per cent gave other reasons. Mothers of children who showed many behaviour problems were more likely to feel that their children prevented them going out:

> Who will babysit — will they cope in an emergency — what if Susan gets in a bad temper and they can't cope?

> Yes he prevents me going out. I can't leave him. You've got to

be two weeks in front of him to know what he's going to get up to next. He wears me out.

It is important to note, however, that there were no differences in the actual frequency of parental outings between those families in which the child had many behaviour problems and those in which the child had few or no problems. Therefore, simply providing parents with breaks from their children and with opportunities for outings will not necessarily increase their satisfaction. Interventions should also help them to feel more positive about their child's behaviour and more capable of dealing with it and understanding it. Parents of children with serious medical problems, on the other hand, might benefit more from knowing that there is someone with the expertise to care for their child if they wish to go out.

Family outings

Although family outings with young children can be a source of pleasure and enjoyment, they can also create difficulties, as described below by Rapoport *et al.* (1977):

> Day-time leisure with small children can also create considerable tension. Many parents find that the interests of very young children do not coincide with the kind of events that they need and enjoy . . . Their noisiness and restlessness, slow pace, rapid fatigue or ceaseless energy, inability to sit still, and numerous similar and conflicting characteristics of young children dampen many parents' enjoyment of leisure activities, and perhaps make them feel that the net balance of pleasure over strain is not positive. (p. 265)

Such difficulties affected many of the families we interviewed. Fifty-two per cent of mothers described difficulties with family outings, including shopping. For 36 per cent, these were reported as minor difficulties and for 16 per cent as major difficulties that prevented family outings almost entirely. Outings that included the children caused difficulties for a larger proportion of families than did parental outings without the children.

When asked about the cause of difficulties, the majority mentioned some aspect of the child's behaviour:

71

I have to watch her when we go visiting. She goes into their cupboards to see if they have anything to eat. She's into everything, and is very strong-willed too.

Only two mothers cited the child's health as a reason and one referred to the reaction of others to the child. Six mothers mentioned problems unrelated to the child. Those mothers who perceived their children as having many behaviour problems felt that these restricted family outings. However, there were no differences according to the number of behaviour problems actually shown by the child:

It's all work wherever you take him.

This links up with one of the findings of Study 4: Family relationships and the children's behaviour, where a small group of mothers described their children as being difficult to manage, yet their children did not have more behaviour problems than others who were not described in this way by their mothers. This group had poor relationships with their children, expressed little affection towards them and were likely to have high Malaise scores. There is likely to be considerable overlap between this group of mothers and the group who felt that their children's difficult behaviour prevented family outings. It would seem reasonable to conclude that a critical factor here is mothers' adjustment to the child. For this group, counselling about their relationships and feelings towards the child would seem to be of benefit, along with practical help.

For almost half of the families, the children caused no restrictions to family outings:

Oh yes, we can take him out. I like to go shopping with him because we usually go and have a 'naughty but nice' cake, as he says.

She does what we do really.

Family holidays

Table 5.4 presents the frequency of holidays for the families in the cohort. Of the seven per cent of families who had never been on holiday, all mentioned reasons unrelated to the child, mostly lack

Table 5.4: Frequency of holidays

Frequency	% of families
More than once a year	21
Annual holidays	48
Holidays every 2/3 years	16
Holidays less frequently/never	15

of money. Of those who had been on holiday, the majority described these as successful (77 per cent). Only seven per cent referred to the child's behaviour as contributing to the lack of success of the holiday. A number of mothers said that they planned their choice of holiday carefully in order to ensure that all family members could enjoy themselves:

> I like Pontins (holiday camp) because it's closed in, you know what I mean, it doesn't matter if she gets lost. So it gives me a break . . . and it gives her a break, 'cause she can do her own thing.

Thirteen per cent of families had been on holiday at least once without the child with Down's syndrome, because they felt that the whole family needed a break:

> We go for the sake of the other children, so we can spend time with them.

In summary, over half of the women we interviewed were content with all of the aspects of family leisure covered. However, one quarter rarely went out with their husbands without the children. These were more likely to be the parents of children with serious medical problems and they perceived a need for experienced, reliable child minders. Thirty-eight per cent of mothers would have liked to go out more with their husbands but only 15 per cent felt it was the problems of the child with Down's syndrome that prevented this. Fifty-two per cent described difficulties with family outings. Mothers who perceived their children as being difficult were more likely to feel that family outings were restricted. This appears to indicate difficulties in the mother–child relationship and in adjusting to the child. For most families, family holidays were successful and they were often deliberately planned with the child in mind.

Relationships between the parents

Rapoport *et al.* (1977) reach the following conclusion about families of non-handicapped children in the early and middle years of parenting:

> A number of studies are now available which document that the myth of happy families in this phase is really only applicable to a proportion of couples, a proportion that declines for each year of marriage until the children have left home. (p. 230)

This feeling of reduced satisfaction is much more pronounced for wives than for husbands and appears to be related to the strain of coping with the conflicting needs and demands of different family members (Bernard, 1975). It is possible that parents of children with disabilities may have additional and unfamiliar demands placed on them and may thus experience even more strain on their relationships. The evidence for this is mixed. Friedrich and Friedrich (1981) found that parents of children with learning difficulties experience significantly less marital satisfaction than parents of non-handicapped children. However, other researchers have found no differences in marital satisfaction (e.g. Waisbren, 1980). These different findings may be due to differences in the ages of the children, in the nature or severity of their disabilities or the way in which marital satisfaction is rated. A number of review studies conclude that the divorce rate is no higher in parents of children with learning difficulties (Longo and Bond, 1984; McConachie, 1986). This indicates that whatever the difficulties, they are just as likely as other couples to remain together.

Where the marital relationship remains strong, it can serve as a resource that helps parents to cope with difficulties. For example, Friedrich (1979) found that marital satisfaction in families of children with learning difficulties was the best overall predictor of successful coping behaviour and low stress. Nihira, Meyers and Mink (1980) concluded that the strength of the parents' marital relationship was related to the adjustment of families to learning difficulties. Beckman (1983) and German and Maisto (1982) found that distress in mothers was much less when there were two parents present in the home.

We have already explored some aspects of the marital relationship in the first part of this chapter. We found that although sharing of household and child-care tasks was relatively low, only 19 per cent of the mothers said they would like more help from their husbands and/or children. Satisfaction with the extent to which parents could go out alone together was somewhat lower (62 per cent), although again, the majority of mothers were content. In this section, we explore the process of decision-making with regard to the child with Down's syndrome, as another way of gaining some insight into the relationship between parents. We describe the ratings we made of the quality of the marital relationships and compare these to other studies. Finally, we describe the effect that mothers in the cohort felt the child with Down's syndrome had on their marital relationships. It is important to remember that all of the views expressed here are mothers' views and fathers' views may differ from these.

With regard to making decisions about the child with Down's syndrome, these were shared in 61 per cent of families. Where one person tended to make the decision, it was more often the mother (32 per cent of families) than the father (three per cent).

He's the chairman, I'm the managing director . . .

I rule the children and he rules everything else, you know . . . it's just on a give and take basis.

I have them both in line, husband and son.

The proportion who tended to agree on most decisions (61 per cent) is similar to that reported by Carr (1975) in families of young children with Down's syndrome (67 per cent). Where there were disagreements between parents in the cohort, these were most frequently about discipline, followed by decisions about schooling, followed by decisions about short-term care. Two per cent of mothers reported that fathers took no part in decisions about the child, and four per cent were single parents.

In most families. there were some differences in child management between mothers and fathers. In 40 per cent of families, mothers felt they were more strict and in 27 per cent, they felt that the fathers were more strict:

Yes, he (the husband) hasn't got as much confidence in him as I have, so he doesn't let him do as much as I do.

I'm the disciplinarian in this house. I'm the rotten one. And then he'll (the husband) say to me 'Will you tell her?'

These proportions are similar to those given by Newson and Newson (1968) for parents of non-handicapped, four-year-old children.

As part of Study 4: Family relationships and the children's behaviour, ratings of the marital relationships were made, based on the work of Richman *et al.* (1982). During the course of the interview, the interviewer noted the warmth and affection with which the wife spoke of her husband, the positive or negative remarks she made about him and the presence or absence of quarrels or arguments. The relationship was rated on what was actually said, on tone of voice, on facial expression and on other aspects of non-verbal behaviour. A rating of 'good' was made when there were marked expressions of warmth, affection, mutual satisfaction and enjoyment of each other's company. A rating of 'average' indicated some tensions and quarrels along with expressions of warmth and concern. A rating of 'poor' was made when warmth, concern and enjoyment of each other's company was almost completely absent and there was a high level of rows and disagreements. A rating of 'very poor' indicated a separation within the last three months or open antagonism and dislike with no positive aspects. Ratings made in this way have been validated by follow-up studies, which showed much higher rates of subsequent divorce and separation in marriages rated 'poor' or 'very poor' (Quinton *et al.*, 1976; Richman *et al.*, 1982). Within our study, percentage agreement on 20 interviews in which the marital relationships were rated by two raters was 100 per cent.

Twenty-eight per cent of the marriages of the parents of children with Down's syndrome who took part in Study 4 were rated as 'good'. The majority (65 per cent) were rated as 'average'. Six per cent were rated as 'poor' and one per cent as 'very poor'. This compares very favourably with the figures given by Richman *et al.* (1982), where 22 per cent of the marriages of mothers of three-year-old, non-handicapped children were rated as either 'poor' or 'very poor'. The figures for the same sample when the children were four and eight years old were 28 per cent and 24 per cent respectively.

The differences between the two groups of families in the marital ratings may be due to a number of differences between the groups apart from the differences in the ages of the children and the presence or absence of a child with Down's syndrome. In the Richman *et al.* (1982) sample there were fewer families who owned their own homes, many more families who lived in flats, fewer fathers with further education, and fewer employed mothers. Some of these factors suggest more difficulties affecting these families and the marital relationships of the parents. However, the important conclusion to be drawn is that there does not appear to be a direct relationship between having a child with Down's syndrome in the family and the marriage suffering.

In her interview study of mothers of children with Down's syndrome between birth and two years, Gath (1973) found that significantly more marriages were rated as 'poor' than in a control group of mothers of non-handicapped children of the same age. However, there were no significant differences between the number of marriages rated as 'good' in the two groups. These two groups were followed up when the children were eight to nine years old (Gath and Gumley, 1984). By this time, there were no significant differences in marital ratings between the groups. It may be that soon after the birth of a child with Down's syndrome, the marital relationship is under great strain and that this eases as the couple adapt to their situation, although the strain may increase again as the child grows up. It seems likely, also, that the impact on the marriage will be influenced by many factors, such as the social and material circumstances of the family, the support they receive and the other difficulties with which they may be coping.

Returning to Study 3: The child, the family and the community, we asked the women who were interviewed for this study how they felt their marriages had changed since the birth of the child with Down's syndrome. Their replies are shown in Table 5.5. Mothers'

Table 5.5: Influence of the child with Down's syndrome on the marriage

	% of familes
Better	30
No change	37
Better in some ways, worse in others	15
Worse	14
Single-parent family	4

replies were not found to be related to their child's age, health or position in the family. There was also no significant variation due to social class or to the number of behaviour problems shown by the child. Those women whose children were less socially able were more likely to feel that their marital relationship had deteriorated.

The same was true of women who *felt* that their children had many behaviour problems. Similarly, and as might be expected, those who felt that the child prevented them having time to themselves also felt that the child had influenced the marriage adversely.

The small group of women who felt that their marriages had deteriorated, appear to overlap with the group described in previous sections, who felt that their lives were restricted and their children were difficult. This group had poor relationships with their children and poor adaptation to the disability. They experienced high levels of stress.

Sixty-seven per cent of mothers felt that their relationships with their husbands had either improved or remained the same:

She helped us a lot in our marriage — it didn't start properly 'till we had Jane.

It made us more aware of each other and how we feel.

These figures for the cohort are in marked contrast to those of Pahl and Quine (1984) where 40 per cent of mothers of children with severe learning difficulties said their marriages had deteriorated and only 25 per cent that it had improved. The contrast with Lonsdale (1978) is even greater. In her sample, 28 per cent of mothers felt that their marriages had not been affected, 17 per cent recorded an improvement and 55 per cent felt the relationship had been strained.

This difference between the cohort and the studies of Lonsdale (1978) and Pahl and Quine (1984) could be due to a number of different factors. It could be due to differences in how the mothers perceive their children. Those children in the cohort whose mothers felt that they had many behaviour problems or that they were less socially able, were more likely to be perceived as placing a strain on the marital relationship. Variation in the ages of the children, the extent of their disabilities, the duration of the marriages or the level of support received by families may also account for the differences between the studies. A further factor relates to the bias towards social classes I and II among the families in the cohort. The difference could be due to their better social and material circumstances.

The most important conclusion to draw from the different studies is that the relationship between parents will not inevitably suffer because of a child with learning difficulties. Indeed, for the families in the cohort, this does not seem any more likely than for families of non-handicapped children.

Mothers' feelings and views

Families do not react passively to events. They work to make sense of the event and its potential impact on their lives. Having appraised the situation, they then deal with it, using the resources at their disposal (Folkman, Schaefer and Lazarus, 1979; McCubbin, Joy, Cauble, Comeau, Patterson and Needle, 1980; Pearlin and Schooler, 1978). The sense which people make of events, both stressful and otherwise, depends on their beliefs and values. In turn, these beliefs and values may be altered by the outcome that results from dealing with the event. For example, the family's beliefs and attitudes about learning difficulties may be central to the coping strategies they evolve and may change as a result of those strategies (Byrne and Cunningham, 1985; Crnic *et al.*, 1983a; Turnbull *et al.*, 1986).

In this section, we explore the ways in which women in the cohort felt that they dealt with the birth of their child with Down's syndrome. We examine some of the beliefs that they expressed to the interviewers about learning difficulties and about the ways in which they had changed since the birth of their children.

As shown in Chapter 4, almost all of the women in the cohort took great pride and pleasure in their children as individuals. As one way of exploring how they had made sense of having a child with Down's syndrome and how they had coped with this, we asked mothers what advice they would give to a mother in a similar situation. Their replies are shown in Table 5.6. Twelve per cent of mothers said they couldn't give advice as every situation was different. The quotes below illustrate some of the strategies they advised:

You think it's the end of the world. It's not. There are people who will help and support you. Go and see another mother.

I would tell her it's got to get better. They're just like normal kids, but they take a little bit longer.

Don't listen to professionals. Don't accept what they tell you, it's not true. Your child is an unknown quantity.

Your child will bring far more happiness than you dream. Take it home, love it and work with it.

Table 5.6: *Advice to new mothers of infants with Down's syndrome*

Advice	% of mothers
Reassurance	
— it's not as bad as you think	26
— the baby will bring joy	8
Advice on how to treat the child	
— treat as normal	17
— stimulate and teach the child	9
General advice	
— on services and benefits	14
— don't make plans — live a day at a time	2
— face up to the handicap	2
— you don't have to keep the baby	1

The strategy of living one day at a time and not making plans is one that was adopted by many more than the two per cent of mothers presented in Table 5.6. When we asked mothers what their aspirations were for their children and whether or not they had made plans for the future, 42 per cent had made some plans and 35 per cent said they just didn't look ahead. They expressed great anxiety and uncertainty about the future for their children. Of those who did look ahead, 26 per cent hoped for an integrated, independent future. They spoke of further education, open employment, independent living and a 'normal' social life. Ten per cent hoped for a sheltered future with other people with learning difficulties and 24 per cent spoke of some mixture of these two.

The majority of women felt that their views about learning difficulties had changed since the child was born (85 per cent). Fifty-six per cent said that they were less fearful of people with learning difficulties and knew how to interact with them more. Thirty-six per cent were more aware of their unmet needs and the discrimination that exists against them. Thirty per cent said that they valued people with learning difficulties more, and felt that they had a contribution to make:

I'm less embarrassed now. I don't shy away as much. I'm more aware of what might be hurtful.

I realise they are people with feelings, likes and dislikes, just like anyone else.

Before I wasn't aware that they could be an important member of the family.

The majority of women (74 per cent) also felt that they them-selves had changed since the birth of the child with Down's syn-drome. The directions of these changes are indicated in Table 5.7.

Table 5.7: Ways in which mothers felt they had changed

	% of mothers
Less concerned with trivia	33
Less materialistic	23
Appreciate health more	15
Less self-centred	10
Value appearance/ability less	6
Self-concept enhanced	3

All of the changes cited were positive ones:

I think I'm more of an all-round person now. I've got a more open outlook on life.

I've got things in proportion now . . . I'll never hit bottom as deep again. She and the family unit are all that matter and life is precious.

It forced me to realise how vulnerable we all are, especially the handicapped.

I've re-evaluated what is important. Before, I would have thought that someone with little academic ability was less of a person.

I'm not as ambitious as I was . . . health is the most important thing in life.

Finally, as one way of assessing the effects on mothers, we asked them to complete the Malaise Inventory (Rutter *et al.*, 1970). This is a 24-item, yes/no questionnaire that taps anxiety, depression and psychosomatic concerns. For example, 'Do you often feel miserable or depressed?' / 'Are you frightened of going out alone or of meeting people?' It has been widely used in British studies to measure the effects of potentially stressful events or circumstances. It has also been used to measure depression. In Table 5.8, the average Malaise score of mothers in the cohort is compared to other studies of mothers of children with learning difficulties and non-handicapped children. Rutter *et al.* (1970) state that a Malaise

Table 5.8: Comparisons of Malaise scores

Studies	Mean	SD	N
Bradshaw and Lawton (1978)	9.0	5.2	303
Burden (1980)	6.1	5.1	25
The cohort: Study 3	4.5	4.1	103
The cohort: Study 4	4.2	3.8	120
Quine and Pahl (1985)	5.8	4.1	200
Rutter (1970)	3.2	(Isle of Wight)	
	4.15	(London)	

score above 5 is outside the normal range and is indicative of depression. Thirty per cent of the mothers we interviewed scored above this cut-off point. This is much lower than the 59 per cent of mothers of children with severe learning difficulties interviewed by Quine and Pahl (1985) who scored above the cut-off point, as is the average Malaise score (Table 5.8). The average score is also much lower than that found by Bradshaw and Lawton (1978) in their study of parents of children with severe disabilities who had applied to the Family Fund. It is also lower than that found by Burden (1980) for parents of infants with severe disabilities. Quine and Pahl (1985) found that the mean Malaise score of parents of children with Down's syndrome was the same as the mean score for their whole sample, which included many different conditions. They conclude that stress levels, as measured by the Malaise Inventory are not related to the child's condition. The average score for mothers in the cohort is similar to that of mothers in London in the original study (Rutter *et al.*, 1970).

These results suggest better mental health and less stress in the cohort mothers than in other groups of mothers of children with disabilities. They also indicate that stress is not inevitable for mothers of children with learning difficulties. This is not due to the early intervention service received by the cohort families as the control group of mothers who participated in Study 4, and who did not receive this service, had similar Malaise scores to cohort mothers. The next section will describe those factors that are related to maternal stress.

Factors related to maternal stress and satisfaction

In previous chapters, we have considered the factors associated with different measures of outcome for the children with Down's syndrome. In this section we consider the factors associated with outcome for their mothers. We know that 30 per cent of mothers scored above the cut-off point on the Malaise Inventory and thus experienced high levels of stress. We also know that a substantial minority (between a quarter and a half) were dissatisfied with various aspects of their daily lives and relationships — some wanted more help at home or more time to themselves, some felt that outings alone with their husbands or family outings were restricted and some felt that their marriages had deteriorated. In order to suggest the amount and type of support such families need, we need to determine who they are, whether they have difficulties in more than one area and what factors are associated with the difficulties.

We looked first at maternal stress, using the Malaise score as the measure. We examined the relationship between all of the child, parent and family characteristics listed in Table 3.11 and maternal stress using the same process as that described in Chapters 3 and 4. The results of this series of analyses indicated that three characteristics are associated with a high Malaise score and thus with anxiety, depression and distress:

(1) Child behaviour problems — the mothers of children who showed many behaviour problems tended to have high scores on the Malaise Inventory.
(2) Parental education — maternal Malaise scores tended to be lowest in those families where both parents had further education.
(3) Sibling relationships — maternal Malaise scores tended to be highest in those families where relationships between the children were poor.

Scores on the Malaise Inventory tended to remain similar over time. For 44 mothers who participated in both Study 3 and Study 4, 34 scored within two points of their original rating on the second occasion.

In the second series of analyses, we looked at maternal satisfaction. We combined the answers to all those interview questions that asked how happy mothers were, or whether they wished to change various aspects of their lives. A woman with a high rating on this measure of satisfaction felt that: she had enough time to herself; she had enough help in the home; outings with her husband, family outings and holidays were satisfactory; relationships with her husband, with the extended family and with friends had not deteriorated; and her plans had not been restricted. A low rating indicated the opposite. One characteristic was significantly related to this measure — family-sharing — maternal satisfaction tended to be highest where tasks and decision-making were shared between all family members. The measure of maternal satisfaction was significantly correlated with the Malaise score. Mothers with a high Malaise score, indicating depression and distress, not surprisingly, expressed dissatisfaction with many aspects of their lives.

The relationship with parental education could be explained in a number of ways. Firstly, education level is associated with social class, employment and financial circumstances. It is not surprising that these factors should be related to maternal distress. We know from Chapter 4 that such factors are related to child-behaviour problems both in the children considered here and in non-handicapped children. A second reason could be that families who have had fewer educational opportunities may be less able to seek out professional help or advice and less able to communicate with the providers of such help.

The relationship between child-behaviour problems, family relationships and maternal stress and satisfaction is supported by similar analyses that we carried out as part of Study 4: family relationships and the children's behaviour. This analysis showed that a subgroup of mothers had high Malaise scores, low mother–child relationship scores and low Judson scores (indicating poor adjustment to the child). This subgroup had children with significantly higher behaviour problem scores than other children. The difficulties in behaviour seemed to consist of socially intrusive behaviours, for example, discipline problems, attention-seeking, poor relationships, concentration problems, etc. There also appeared to be relationship problems within the family as a whole, both marital difficulties and difficulties between the parents and other children in the family. It is not possible to say which of these factors causes the others. However, it is important to be aware that where one is found, the others are likely to be present. They signify difficulties for all family members.

Summary

This chapter moves away from a direct consideration of the child with Down's syndrome to focus on other aspects of the family unit. Three aspects are explored: (1) how the families in the cohort managed child-care and household tasks and how they met the social and recreational needs of family members; (2) the parents' marital relationships; (3) some of the ways in which the mothers we interviewed felt they had changed since the birth of their children. Finally, the factors associated with maternal stress and satisfaction are described.

Most housework and child care was carried out by mothers with little help from anyone else. They received most help with minding and entertaining the children and least help with housework. This pattern is typical, regardless of whether or not there is a child with learning difficulties in the family. Fathers helped more than anyone else and most women were content with the help they received from their husbands. However, half of the women we interviewed said they would like more help from some source and that they would like more time to themselves.

Over half of the women interviewed were content with all aspects of family leisure. However, one quarter rarely went out with their husbands without the children. These were more likely to be the parents of children with serious medical problems, who felt a need for experienced child minders on whom they could rely. Thirty-eight per cent of mothers were dissatisfied with the frequency of these outings and 52 per cent described difficulties with family outings. Mothers who perceived their children as being difficult to manage were more likely to feel that family outings were restricted. These were not necessarily those children with many behaviour problems. For most families, family holidays were successful and they were often deliberately planned with the child in mind.

Only seven per cent of marital relationships in the cohort were rated as 'poor' or 'very poor', a much smaller proportion than in families of non-handicapped children in London (Richman *et al.*, 1982). Most women felt that their marriages had either remained unchanged or improved since the birth of the child with Down's syndrome. Mothers who felt that their relationships had deteriorated were again more likely to be those who felt that their children were difficult to manage. Also, mothers who rated their children as less socially able were more likely to feel that their marriages had deteriorated. The marital relationship does not inevitably suffer in families with a child with learning difficulties and, indeed, may be less likely to be strained than in families of non-handicapped children.

The majority of mothers felt that their attitudes to learning difficulties and their priorities in general had improved since the birth of their children. Their average Malaise score was comparable to mothers of non-handicapped children, although 30 per cent did score above the cut-off point, indicating depression and distress.

These findings indicate that between a quarter and a half of mothers were distressed and unhappy with various aspects of their lives. The factors associated with maternal distress and dissatisfaction were: behaviour difficulties in the children with Down's syndrome; family-relationship difficulties, both in terms of difficulties between siblings and a lack of sharing within the family; and low parental education.

We already know from Chapter 3 that behaviour difficulties are associated with difficulties for the children with Down's syndrome themselves in their activities and their relationships with friends and siblings. We know from Chapter 4 the factors that are associated with behaviour difficulties. We know too that behaviour difficulties are likely to persist as are high maternal Malaise scores. It is thus vital that the families who are vulnerable should receive help as early as possible. Vulnerable families are the same as those identified in Chapter 4. There appears to be a cluster of difficulties that are associated with one another, although it is not possible to say which are causal. Different difficulties may occur first in different families and then lead to the others.

Vulnerable families are those who are subject to extra stresses such as unemployment and poor education. They are also families where the child with Down's syndrome has more severe learning difficulties. Services in the form of benefits and advice should be directed to these families in particular. The services should be provided in a form that the families can use — one that fits in with the family culture and style.

A second group of vulnerable families are those where the mother – child relationship is poor and the mother may have found it difficult to adjust to the child's condition. In these families, levels of maternal stress are high, the child is regarded as presenting management difficulties and the mother feels restricted and isolated. This suggests that maternal beliefs and self-concept may influence attachment to the child and perception of the child and of the child's behaviour.

The most vulnerable group of families appear to be those few where poor mother – child relationships reflect poor family relationships generally. There is a lack of family sharing and the child's behaviour is socially intrusive, consisting of attention-seeking, poor relationships, difficulties in concentrating, etc. The behaviour difficulties of these children are not related to low developmental level but to family-interrelationship difficulties. These latter two groups of families require a very different intervention, directed not to the child's behaviour but to relationships within the family. Intervention should begin soon after the birth of the child with Down's syndrome. The framework and skills needed to identify such families and to work with them will be identified and discussed in later chapters.

Finally, it is important to note that these difficulties do not apply to all of the families in the cohort. For the majority, family life was not very different to that in families of non-handicapped children.

6

The Families: Relatives, Friends and other Families

> Just as the family is a support system for individuals, social networks are support systems for families and individual members. This view stresses the importance of kin, friends and neighbours in the informal exchanges of human services which form so much of family life. These exchanges centre on *personal* involvements in offering help, advice, affection, and responsiveness to norms and values. It is distinguished from the supports given by more formal specialists and organisations based on cash payments or statutory obligations — e.g. doctors, counsellors, schools and governmental agencies.
>
> (Rapoport, Fogarty and Rapoport, 1982, p. 486)

We acknowledge that the family unit does not exist in isolation. Each family member has relationships with people outside the immediate family. These may be relatives, close friends, neighbours, acquaintances, colleagues at work, other members of clubs and institutions to which the family member belongs and other people seen regularly. All of these people constitute the family member's social network. This network may vary in the number and variety of people it contains, the closeness, depth and duration of relationships within it, the extent to which friends are shared by different family members and the extent to which network members know each other. Independently of all of these features, people may also vary in the extent to which they feel isolated and in the extent to which they feel supported by their social networks.

There is an enormous body of research literature that indicates that the support provided by one's social network can protect people from the harmful effects of stress (for reviews see Gottlieb,

1981; Haggerty, 1980). The types of problems which have been studied include the stress resulting from divorce, depression, cancer, birth complications, job dissatisfaction, job loss, child abuse and many others. There is also evidence that social support enhances family functioning and well-being (Bott, 1971; McCubbin *et al.*, 1980). It influences attitudes towards parenting, styles of parenting and therefore also influences child behaviour and development (Crnic, Greenberg, Ragozin, Robinson and Basham, 1983b; Crockenberg, 1981).

Support networks act in three ways to protect against the harmful effects of stress and influence psychological well-being: they provide practical help, information and emotional empathy and understanding (Crnic *et al.*, 1983b). A further role of social networks, not often considered in the research literature, is that they enhance well-being by providing opportunities for relaxation, escape and entertainment. In all of these ways, this framework of support helps people to feel cared for and valued and part of a network of mutual obligation (Cobb, 1976). According to Gourash (1978), the support provided by members of the social network means that families do not have to seek help from professionals. If professional services become necessary, members of the social network may 'act as screening and referral agents' and 'transmit attitudes, values and norms about help-seeking' (p. 516).

With regard to families of children with learning difficulties, support networks may not be able to fulfil all of these functions. Relatives and friends may feel that they lack the information and knowledge to provide either advice or practical help. They may feel embarrassed and thus avoid the family. Grandparents and other relatives may themselves be finding it hard to adapt to the presence of a child with learning difficulties, and may be unable to support the parents and siblings of the child (Stagg and Catron, 1986). Parents may feel that they cannot ask for help because they do not have the time or resources to help in return. Networks may then become a source of strain (e.g. Waisbren, 1980; Kazak and Marvin, 1984). Social networks may change after the birth of a child with learning difficulties, and may come to include families of children with similar difficulties. Professional services may be needed both to support the family, and to provide the information and skills to enable the informal network to help.

Although there have been a number of studies examining social support in families of children with learning difficulties, no clear conclusions can be drawn from them. Some studies have found that such families have less support available to them than families of non-handicapped children (e.g. Friedrich and Friedrich, 1981). Others (e.g. Stagg and Catron, 1986) found no differences in any dimension of social networks. However, Stagg and Catron did find differences in mothers' perceptions of the quality of their support. Furthermore, these differences were related to the age of the child. Mothers of younger children with learning difficulties (birth to six years) were less satisfied with the support they received than mothers of non-handicapped children of the same age. There were no differences between mothers of children with learning difficulties and mothers of non-handicapped children from six to twelve years of age. On the other hand, mothers of teenagers with learning difficulties were more satisfied with the support they received than mothers of non-handicapped teenagers. Thus it may be that the findings depend on which aspect of social support is measured at which stage of the family life-cycle.

Recently, a number of researchers have questioned the theoretical basis, the definitions and the methods used to study social support (e.g. Alloway and Bebbington, 1987; Barrera, 1986; Coyne and DeLongis, 1986; Starker, 1986). They argue that: 'concepts are fuzzy in this field, definitions are rare, measurement methods are inconsistent and research designs have been weak.' (Cobb and Jones, 1984, p. 48.) Researchers are moving away from the view that more social support inevitably means better psychological well-being, and are beginning to define more clearly which aspects of social support they are studying.

In this chapter, we confine ourselves to two aspects of social support. We describe the types of assistance that the cohort families received from three potential sources: members of their extended families, their friends and other mothers of children with learning difficulties. We then describe mothers' perceptions of being supported by their social networks and their satisfaction with this.

Sources of support: relatives and friends

In Chapter 5, we noted that as far as help with daily household and child-care tasks was concerned, support from the extended family and friends was negligible. In this section, we explore the support that families did receive from these sources.

We asked mothers which relatives provided help or support.

More support was received from the mother's than from the father's family. Approximately twice as many women cited their own families as sources of support as cited their husband's families. In both families, it was the grandmothers who were most frequently described as sources of support, with the maternal grandmother cited by 56 per cent of women. In Study 4: Family relationships and the children's behaviour, when we asked about frequency of contact, we found that 59 per cent of families saw the maternal grandparents at least once per week, whereas only 28 per cent saw the paternal grandparents at least once per week. Grant (1984) also found, in his study of families caring for adult members with learning difficulties, that more support was received from the mothers' than from the fathers' families. This situation, of families having more contact with maternal than paternal grandparents, applies also to families with non-handicapped children.

It is important to remember that our studies describe mothers' views and that the social networks of husbands and wives may be quite different (Schilling, Schinke and Kirkham, 1985). For example, Waisbren (1980) concluded that for fathers of developmentally delayed infants, their relationships with their parents was more important than all other sources of support.

Table 6.1: Type of help provided by relatives and friends

Type of help	% Families	
	Relatives	Friends
Practical help	30	13
Emotional support	9	20
Both practical and emotional support	46	38
No help or support	15	29

Table 6.1 presents the types of support provided by the extended family and by friends. From both sources, the most frequent type of practical help given was child-minding, either during the day or in the evening. Minding the children overnight was much less frequent and was done more often by relatives (11 per cent) than by friends (one per cent). As we have already noted, help with household and child-care tasks was minimal.

Emotional support consisted of listening, being a good friend and having a helpful attitude. Advice was rarely cited as a form of support. Only two per cent of the women we interviewed mentioned receiving advice from relatives, and four per cent from friends. They were more likely to receive practical help from relatives than from friends, and received emotional support equally from both sources. Relatives were more likely to provide support of some kind than were friends. These findings are very similar to those of Cooke and Lawton (1984) in their study of a nationally representative sample of families with disabled children, and to those of Ayer and Alaszewski (1984) who interviewed mothers of children with severe learning difficulties.

The quotations below illustrate the range of support received by the women we interviewed and some opinions of that support:

My parents take us out in the car, come and visit. They're great at birthdays, and they babysit for the whole day.

(Friends.) We take turns to mind each other's children, go out together with the children. I can talk to them. I've known them for years.

(Friends.) If I asked, they would be there. I don't always need it, but it's nice to know.

(Maternal grandparents.) We live back to back, they have her all the time. We're a very close-knit family.

Relatives should offer instead of me having to ask. I always feel as if we are causing problems.

I've never asked for help or needed it. I want to be independent.

Support from family and friends did not vary significantly with marital status, the age of the child, the health of the child or the ability of the child. However, all four single-parent families in the cohort felt supported by both relatives and friends. This is similar to the findings of Dunst, Trivette and Cross (1986), who concluded that the absence of support from a partner was, in part, compensated for by support from other sources. In our study, we reached a similar conclusion with regard to the husbands' employment status.

Relatives were most supportive in families in which the husbands were employed and were frequently absent from home as part of their work. This was possibly compensation for the lack of support from the husband due to his absences. In families where

Table 6.2: Changes in relationships with relatives and friends

| | % Families | |
	Relatives	Friends
Not changed	57	82
Better	27	7
Worse	16	11

the husband was unemployed, and therefore more available at home, we found that mothers felt significantly less supported by relatives. Support from friends did not differ according to the employment status of the husband.

Mothers who were older when their child with Down's syndrome was born were more likely to feel supported by friends than were younger mothers. This latter finding is again similar to that of Dunst *et al.* (1986) who noted that older mothers were more satisfied with the help they received. This is possibly because older parents have more-established and longstanding networks of friends. They may also have lower expectations of help and support, expecting to cope alone.

We asked mothers whether they felt that their relationships with relatives and friends had changed since the child with Down's syndrome was born (Table 6.2). Relationships with relatives had changed for many more women than had relationships with friends. This was more often due to improvements in the relationships rather than to a deterioration:

My father has become more tolerant, more gentle and understanding. He realises there's a dimension to my life which is ghastly.

I'm closer to my Dad now. He shows his feelings more.

The relationship with my parents has deepened, though we've always been close.

My friends were nervous at first and embarrassed, but it's OK now.

Sources of support: other mothers of children with Down's syndrome

A further potential source of informal support comes from other mothers of children with learning difficulties. With other mothers, it may be that a mother need not fear rejection or embarrassment for herself or her child. She may not have to prepare an explanation of why and how her child is different. She can share experiences, gain more knowledge and feel understood. However, it is also possible that if her only social contacts are with other mothers of children with learning difficulties, there may be less access to other resources and to different viewpoints (e.g. Granovetter, 1973; Hammer, 1983; Kazak and Marvin, 1984).

Most of the women in the cohort had met other mothers of children with Down's syndrome (93 per cent) and the majority found such meetings helpful (75 per cent) because they provided an opportunity to share concerns with others in a similar situation:

> The biggest support is other Mums. You must have a mentally handicapped child to understand and really know the thoughts and problems a mother has.

> It's useful for swapping information about services and agencies. I got a buggy 'cause another mother told me how.

> It's helpful to meet parents of older children and see what yours might achieve.

Other mothers were never described as a source of practical help. Forty-nine per cent of the women we interviewed said they provided emotional support, seven per cent that they provided advice and information and 14 per cent that they provided both. Women who worked full-time outside the home were significantly less likely to feel supported by other mothers than were those who worked part-time or those who had no paid employment. All of the women who were single parents felt supported by other mothers. There were no other differences, according to any of the family or child characteristics we considered, in the extent to which mothers felt supported by this source.

Of those who did not find it helpful to meet other mothers, the reason most frequently given was that children with Down's syndrome are so different, it is not possible to make comparisons (twelve mothers). Others did not find it helpful because they felt that talking did not help (ten):

> I tend to steer clear of parents of handicapped children, which is

a bit weird, but I think if you're living with the problem, why make your life revolve around other people's handicapped children . . . Why make yourself special and different and alter your own social life. I think the best thing is to lead as normal an existence as possible.

I don't need to meet other mothers. I don't have any problems with her.

One way of meeting other mothers of children with learning difficulties is through voluntary associations. Such associations can serve as a supplement to services and to informal support networks. They may be involved in campaigning for service development, in acting as advocates for people with learning difficulties and their families or, in actually providing services. Both the Wolfenden (1978) and Warnock (DES, 1978) Reports emphasised the important role of voluntary associations in providing such support and services. However, most studies have found that only about half of parents belong to an appropriate organisation (e.g. Ayer and Alaszewski, 1984; Bradshaw, Glendinning and Hatch, 1977; Hewett, 1970). In their study of a nationally representative sample of children with disabilities, Cooke and Lawton (1984) describe much lower rates of membership (five to ten per cent). One reason for this discrepancy may be differences in the ages of the children. Bradshaw *et al.* (1977) showed that there was a decline in membership rates for children over six years and especially for children over eleven years. There may also be different rates of membership depending on the child's condition and the organisation concerned.

Membership was much higher in this sample. Seventy-two per cent of families were members of at least one association, and 30 per cent belonged to more than one. Thirty-three per cent were members of local self-help groups, 28 per cent were members of Mencap and 13 per cent belonged to the Down's Syndrome Association. The only characteristic we found to be significantly related to active involvement in one or more associations was social class. Although there was no social-class difference between those families who belonged to one or more associations and those who belonged to none, families from social classes I and II were more likely to be active members of voluntary associations. They were also more likely to find them helpful than families from social classes III to V. This is supported by an interview study by

Ineichen (1986) in which he found that membership of such associations has a heavy middle-class bias. What mothers found most helpful about their membership of these associations was that they helped them keep up-to-date with services and with ideas for helping their children, and that the associations were campaigning for better services:

It's great! We try to find out what is happening locally with services. We're campaigning for extra residential facilities.

We talk about how to manage the problems that crop up. They understand 'cause they have the same problems, and we have a good laugh.

When we asked mothers why they did not belong, the most frequent response was that they felt no need (56 per cent of those who did not belong to any organisation). The second largest group replied that they did not know about the associations (31 per cent). Eight per cent said that they wished to keep family life as normal as possible and two per cent said they felt it would be depressing to belong:

I haven't got enough time to do what I want to do as it is.

I don't want to be lumped together with the mothers of handicapped children.

We've not got round to it. Maybe we will when she's older.

Satisfaction with support

Only three mothers felt that they did not receive support from any of the sources described in the previous sections — from relatives, friends or other mothers of children with Down's syndrome. Fifty-nine (44 per cent) felt that they were supported by all three sources. The issue of how satisfied mothers were with these levels of support was investigated more fully in Study 4: Family relationships and the children's behaviour.

The most obvious finding was the high level of satisfaction expressed. The majority of the women we interviewed (74 per cent) felt that they saw and socialised with enough people. Eighty-five per cent felt that they had enough people to talk things over with, if they had a worry or problem. When asked who they would be most likely to turn to, apart from their husbands, 33 per cent cited a friend, 24 per cent a relative, two per cent one of their older children and 29 per cent cited more than one person. Eleven per cent said that there was no one apart from their husbands, and five per cent cited a professional rather than a member of their social network. In general, 82 per cent of mothers were rated by the interviewers as perceiving that they had 'high' levels of social support:

> My parents live half a mile down the road. They're very suppor-tive indeed, very supportive. We see them two or three times a week. My husband's sister lives in Derbyshire. We're very close. We get on well and the children get on well. We enjoy seeing them . . . I have a particular friend of my own age who I get on very well with. We tend to chat about the children and bringing up the children, and things in general. I discuss things with her . . . I'm very happy with the way things are. If I wanted to see more people, I could do, quite happily. So I don't feel that I'm hard done by or unhappy about my social situation at all.

> There's usually someone who pops in for a chat every day. I don't visit, they visit me.

Fourteen per cent of mothers were rated as perceiving that they had 'moderate' levels of support, and for four per cent, a rating of 'low' perceived support was made. The quote below illustrates that a wide social network does not always lead to a feeling of being supported. It indicates that professionals should not always take 'the smile and the pat answers' literally, that they need to know parents well, to give them time and to allow them the safety to express their real worries and concerns:

> I'm a very private person from a lot of very, very personal points of view. I've never really discussed real worries I have about him (child with Down's syndrome) . . . I'm the one who comes out with the smile and all the pat answers, but if the truth be known, there are things I'd like to say that do worry me about him that really I can't discuss with anybody, or I don't feel I can, I probably could. Because they don't understand.

They're not in a similar situation. How can they understand?

Summary

This chapter describes the support that the cohort families received from their social networks. Two aspects of this support were considered: the amount and types of help that the women in the cohort felt was available from friends, neighbours and other mothers of children with learning difficulties; and their satisfaction with the help they received.

Almost all of the women we interviewed felt that they were helped by at least one of the sources considered. Support came most often from relatives, then friends, and then other mothers. The mothers' relatives were cited most frequently as sources of support. Practical help most often consisted of child-minding and relatives were most likely to provide this. Looking after the children overnight or for longer was rare. Emotional support, which consisted of listening, being a good friend and having a helpful attitude, came equally from all three sources. Advice was most often provided by other mothers of children with learning difficulties. Mothers who worked full-time outside the home were less likely to feel supported by other mothers. Older mothers were more likely to feel supported by friends than younger mothers.

The absence of support from a partner, in single-parent families and in families where partners were often away was, in part, compensated for by support from other relatives. However, where husbands were unemployed, less support was provided by relatives. We know from previous chapters that levels of stress were high in such families and that unemployed husbands did not contribute more to household and child-care tasks. If support from relatives is withdrawn, this is likely to contribute to further difficulties.

Mothers were more likely to feel that their relationships with relatives had changed since the birth of the child with Down's syndrome than their relationships with friends. This was due to improvements in the relationships more often than to deterioration. However, the majority felt that their relationships with both friends and relatives had not changed.

Most of the families in the cohort belonged to at least one voluntary association. However, mothers from social classes I and II were more likely to be active members of such associations and to find them helpful than were mothers in social classes III to V.

They met other mothers through these, found out about services and ways of helping their children and campaigned for improvements in services.

Satisfaction with the levels of support provided by their informal social networks was very high among the women in the cohort. The majority felt that they saw and socialised with enough people and that they had enough people to talk things over with. Eighty-two per cent were rated by the interviewers as having 'high' levels of perceived social support. However, four per cent were rated as having 'low' levels of perceived support and eleven per cent said that there was no one apart from their husbands that they could talk to. Findings from other sections of this chapter suggest that these are likely to be younger mothers from social classes III to V, whose husbands are unemployed. They are thus exposed to many difficulties and are likely to be vulnerable and in need of support from professionals.

7

Professionals and Services (1)

'Parents understandably want a single door leading to assessment, explanation and treatment. They need a co-ordinated service of care, therapy and education, with regular reviews of the child's progress, leading to advice and support.' (Court Committee on Child Health Services (DHSS, 1976, para. 5.11)). It is clear from preceeding chapters that at some stage in their life cycle, most families of children with learning difficulties have needs that can only be met by statutory support services. The extent and type of needs may vary widely from one family to another and from one stage to another within the life cycle of the same family. They may range from needs for information, counselling or advice, to needs for specific services such as respite care, benefits, specialised medical treatment or speech therapy. In this, and the following chapter, we describe the families' experiences of statutory support services and their views about the services they received.

The ideal is where services are tailored to meet the individual needs of families and thus complement the families' own 'structure for coping' (Bayley, 1973). However, this does not always happen. Indeed, for some families, statutory support services may not only fail to meet their needs but may also be an added source of strain: 'contacts with services were a major source of problems (for parents), which often assumed greater importance than problems arising more directly out of the child's handicap.' (Lloyd-Bostock, 1976, p. 325). Some of the possible reasons for this mismatch between family needs and the services offered will be considered here.

The first set of reasons relates to the complexity of the service network. Dealing with this network may require resources of

100

energy, assertiveness and understanding that many families do not have. They may find the number and variety of different service agencies and practitioners confusing. With each agency, they have to establish new ways of working. They may have to establish relationships with specialists with whom families of non-handicapped children may never come in contact (e.g. genetic counsellors, speech therapists, educational psychologists). These include professionals from the social services department, the local education department, the community health service and the district general hospital.

They also experience changes in established relationships with professionals, for example, with a family doctor or a health visitor (Ayer and Alaszewski, 1984). Parents may find that they know more about their child's condition than generic professionals and yet are still in the relatively powerless role of 'patient'. Often, personnel change and each time the professional may 'review the case' for themselves. For the parent, this may mean constantly going back over painful areas, re-examining feelings and reactions.

Reid (1983) found that only one in eight parents of children with severe learning difficulties understands the organisation of services. In 1978, in order to overcome this confusion and overlap of services, and to provide a 'single door leading to assessment, explanation and treatment', the government asked for multidisciplinary teams to be set up (DHSS, 1978). However, a survey carried out by The Campaign for Mentally Handicapped People over three years later (Plank, 1982) concluded that:

> All too often the services available to mentally handicapped people and their families are dependent on the area in which they live. This is now the situation in respect of multidisciplinary teams. Some areas do not have any. Even where they do exist, the service they provide differs widely . . . They do not ensure that all mentally handicapped people have an equal chance to benefit from an integrated service. (p. 28)

This lack of an integrated service, or even a common service philosophy, means that regardless of skills, a professional may be prevented from being effective. One professional does not know what others are doing or planning for a family, or may even be denied access to families who could benefit from his/her skills because other professionals are unaware of those skills. Reid (1983) found that 90 per cent of families were in favour of having a 'named' person who would act as a link between the family and service agencies, in order to improve access and effectiveness.

At the time of Study 3: The child, the family and the community, community mental-handicap teams did not exist in many areas. Where they did exist, our impression from talking to parents and professionals was that there was often confusion about their roles, especially in providing a service for children. Although community teams have been set up more or less nationally now, this confusion appears to remain (Malin, 1987).

A second set of reasons for the mismatch between family needs and service delivery lies in the training of professionals. As a result of their training, professionals almost inevitably have a different 'worldview' to that of their clients. Cunningham and Davis (1985b) and Darling (1983) describe a number of ways in which the professional role differs from that of a parent of a child with learning difficulties. Such differences can lead to misunderstanding and lack of respect. Firstly, professionals choose their career. They have some choice in whether or not they wish to work with families of children with learning difficulties or with some other client group. Parents have no such choice, unless they are foster or adoptive parents. Secondly, professionals are concerned with many children and their families. Parents are concerned only with their own child. Thirdly, the professional may see the child with learning difficulties as a client or a patient only, or even as 'the child with behaviour problems' or 'the child with a heart condition'. Most professionals dealing with the child will tend to have a specific aim or area of interest set within relatively defined limits. Thus the speech therapist will largely be concerned with the child's communication and the physiotherapist with mobility and posture. Parents, on the other hand, see the child in all his/her different roles, as son or daughter, brother or sister, pupil, friend, grandchild. They may have many areas of concern. Whereas professionals are trained not to be emotionally involved with clients, one of the most important aspects of the parental role is being emotionally involved with their children. This means that parents will have more intense reactions to the total spectrum of the child's behaviour than professionals. It also means that parents are more likely to be persistent advocates for their children.

Finally, the professional is usually in control of any interaction with a parent. The parent may feel powerless and may resent this control. These differing perspectives of professionals and parents may lead to frustration and dissatisfaction on both sides. It is important to consider the extent to which parents can be expected to merge professional and parental skills without inhibiting their enjoyment of their children and their role in providing love and security.

Thus, in order to receive the services they need, the families we interviewed had to learn their way through the network of agencies and then, once in contact with particular professionals, had to relate to them and understand their different roles. In this chapter, we present the range of professionals with whom families were in contact. In particular, we describe the characteristics of different professionals which, in the mothers' view, enabled them together to overcome the difficulties described above. We also describe the characteristics that led to maternal dissatisfaction and anger. Finally, we explore parents' experiences of receiving two specific services: financial assistance and respite care.

Contact with professionals

The families in the cohort were in contact with an average of five professionals (ranging from one to nine professionals) at the time of Study 3. Table 7.1 lists the professionals, the proportions of families in regular contact at the time of the study and the proportions who had been in contact at some time. Home teacher refers to any professional providing a home-teaching service: in certain areas, there was a peripatetic teacher of the deaf who visited children with hearing problems at home; in some areas, a play therapist visited the home; in other areas, a Portage home-teaching service (Bluma, Shearer, Frohman and Hilliard, 1976) was provided by specialist health visitors and others. These services varied widely and were only provided to a minority of families. The professionals referred to are those from statutory agencies only. The early intervention service provided by our research team is therefore not included.

The proportions of families in contact with the various professionals are very similar to those described by Pahl and Quine (1984) in their study of families of children with severe learning difficulties in Kent. The only exceptions are contacts with physiotherapists and child psychologists, with whom fewer families in the cohort were in contact, perhaps due to the different nature of the

Table 7.1: Contact with professionals

Professional[a]	% Families in current contact	% Families who ever had any contact
General practitioner	100	100
Health visitor	62	98
Paediatrician	60	98
Speech therapist	57	68
Audiologist	48	85
Social worker	35	63
Physiotherapist	23	43
Cardiac specialist	16	24
Home teacher	15	30
Psychologist	11	27
Genetic counsellor	2	32

Note: a. This excludes members of the research team who provided the early intervention service.

children's difficulties. Also, in the cohort, more families were in contact with the health visitor, probably because the children were younger at the time of interview. Armstrong *et al.* (1980), in their study of services for the families of children with learning difficulties under five years of age in Leeds and Sheffield, found similar high levels of contact with health visitors. Contact with social workers is low in all of the studies referred to, regardless of the age of the children (e.g. Armstrong *et al.*, 1980; Ayer and Alaszewski, 1984). Within the child's first year, only two out of 47 cohort families had been in contact with a social worker (Cunningham and Sloper, 1977b).

With one exception, the number of professionals with whom families were in contact did not vary with any of the child or family characteristics that we measured. The exception was that families of children with severe health or medical problems were in contact with significantly more professionals than families of children with minor or no problems. There is thus even more need for services to such families to be integrated and co-ordinated. When parents are concerned about their child's health and well-being, they may have even less energy and assertiveness to understand and deal with an even more complex network of professionals. If the child's health is seriously at risk, it is vital that management and treatment plans are not confusing.

Suelze and Keenan (1981) found that the amount of professional support available to families decreased with the increasing age of the children with disabilities. They found that the parents of teenagers and young adults were less supported than parents of younger children. In our earlier work with cohort families, we found a similar decrease within the first year of the child's life. The number of regular visits to the home by the health visitor was highest when the infant was less than three months old (Cunningham, Aumonier and Sloper, 1982). By the time the children were one year old, only 26 per cent of families were visited regularly: (Cunningham *et al.*, 1982). This finding also related to other professionals, with visits from all those in early contact with the family decreasing sharply after the first three months (Cunningham and Sloper, 1977b). This decrease is in frequency and regularity of contact. There is a further decline once the children reach the age of five. At this stage, the decrease is in the number of professionals in contact with the family.

There are a number of reasons for this decrease in contact at the age of five. Contact with health visitors and paediatricians, having become less regular within the first few months of the child's life, usually ceases when the child reaches this age, unless there are particular problems. Home teachers cease to visit the home once the children are attending school. Prior to the child starting school, the educational psychologist may visit the family a number of times to assess the child and to advise the family about the child's educational needs and the schools available in the area. Once the child has settled at school, the psychologist may not visit again unless there are difficulties at school or the child is changing school. If the child attends a special school or unit, many of the services that were provided at home are provided at school. Physiotherapists, speech therapists and psychologists visit children at school. In this way, they can see more children, but parents lose their contact with them and the services they are providing.

This drop in the number of professionals visiting the home may come as a relief to the family. However, it may also mean that parents who are very involved in their child's development, may feel cut off and excluded. At the same time as they are coping with the mixed feelings experienced by all parents when their children start school (Cleave, Jowett and Bate, 1982), they may also lose contact with many professionals. Their role in their child's education and development changes considerably. The relationship between the parents and the school is therefore very important, so that parents may know what is happening to their child and may continue their involvement. This issue is discussed more fully in Chapter 8.

Views about services

In order to find out how services can complement the family's own resources and thus meet their needs, it was not sufficient simply to ask mothers whether or not they found particular professionals helpful. We also asked, about those professionals who were said to be either particularly helpful or particularly unhelpful, what it was about the service they provided that made it so. In this way, we hoped to find out how different professionals managed to overcome the potential difficulties described in the beginning of this chapter.

Table 7.2: Evaluation of services

Professional	Very helpful	OK	Very unhelpful
General practitioner	48	27	25
Health visitor	43	19	38
Paediatrician	43	30	27
Speech therapist	52	35	13
Audiologist	16	71	13
Social worker	56	13	31
Physiotherapist	46	47	7
Cardiac specialist	43	47	10
Home teacher	73	11	16
Psychologist	48	28	24
Genetic counsellor	57	23	20

Table 7.2 lists mothers' evaluations of the different professionals from whom they received services. School teachers are not included, as maternal evaluation of school is explored in Chapter 8. In general, levels of satisfaction were high. Twenty-three per cent of families were in contact with five or more helpful professionals, 56 per cent with between two and five, 14 per cent with one and only six per cent of families were not in contact with any helpful professionals. Approximately half of the women we interviewed (48 per cent) were completely satisfied with all of the services they received. Fifty-two per cent felt that they had at least some needs which were not being met. These views about professionals were based on very different criteria for each of the different professional groups seen. Most women also expressed a high level of consensus in their views and tended to use the same criteria to judge a particular professional group.

Where they found the general practitioners helpful, the largest proportion said that it was because they made themselves available and were prepared to make time:

> The GP is great. He asks about all of the children and doesn't hurry with you.

> He's marvellous. We have his home 'phone number, and can go at any time without an appointment. He knows we're doing the best we can.

Ineichen (1986) reaches a similar conclusion in his review of the service needs of people with learning difficulties living in the community and their families. He notes that what is valued is availability and approachability. Similarly, in our earlier work, when the children were less than one year old, we found that mothers valued their GP's understanding, acceptance and interest in the infant, even if they admitted a lack of knowledge (Cunningham and Sloper, 1977b). Where the GP was found by mothers in the cohort to be particularly unhelpful, the largest proportion said that it was because of 'negative, pessimistic attitudes'.

> He never came near us once we had been told she had Down's syndrome. I think he's embarrassed.

The most frequent criticism of paediatricians, cardiac specialists and audiologists was similarly for their negative attitudes and their lack of helpfulness:

> He (the paediatrician) uses her as a guinea pig and asks me the same old questions every time.

They were most frequently praised for their efficiency and for actually helping. Genetic counsellors were particularly valued for their 'positive, hopeful attitude', and criticised when mothers felt they were being patronised.

Where a professional was seen by mothers as providing a specific intervention to help their children's development, e.g. physiotherapist, speech therapist, psychologist or home teacher, their criticisms were most often based on the lack of effectiveness of the intervention:

> His talking hasn't come on at all since he's been seeing her (the speech therapist).

107

He (the psychologist) was no help. He said, 'Don't smack her. Just speak to her in a calm voice'. That made no difference.

Of course, such criticisms may relate not only to the effectiveness of the intervention made by the professional concerned, but may also reflect the parents' lack of understanding of the professional's role and the possibilities for 'improvement'. However, in such instances, the responsibility for falsely raising parents' expectations lies with the professional or with the referring agent and *not* with the parent. Where the parent saw the intervention as succeeding *or* where the professional involved the parent in teaching the child, this was seen as particularly helpful:

She (the physiotherapist) gave us tips about helping him to crawl, then walk.

She (the home teacher) taught me how to teach, how to break tasks down, and she came every week.

This psychologist has been coming. What happened was, we had a star chart system and I was very doubtful that I didn't think it would be enough incentive for him but it worked absolute wonders. What worked the wonders really, if I'm honest, is that I got somebody checking up on me, if you see what I mean. Because he was going to come back a week later or a fortnight later and I was going to give him a report, so I had to stick to this sending back to bed . . . It taught me that I had to be consistent. It gave me the confidence not to give in to him, that problems can be worked out.

The most valuable contribution of health visitors and social workers was their effective liaison with other services and professionals. They were also praised for taking the trouble to find things out when they did not know. The following comments were made about health visitors:

She's gone out of her way to sort out problems.

She's great, makes sure I get everything I need.

She was really good. She didn't know a lot, but she read up about it. She was a good support.

You can ask her anything.

The comments about social workers are similar:

> He's a decent bloke. He's available and he gives his time. He's helped us to get grants and benefits.

> If I ever have a problem, I just get on the 'phone. She organised a one-to-one play scheme in the holidays.

> She always follows up queries about benefits and things. She took me to visit different schools before John started, and she organised the home-from-home scheme.

> He's on the end of a 'phone.

Health visitors were most often criticised for not knowing enough about Down's syndrome and not finding out. Cunningham *et al.* (1982) conclude that even though many mothers liked and appreciated their health visitors, they still felt that they did not help with practical problems. They expected health visitors to know what to do, or to find out:

> She (the health visitor) was a nice lady, but she was in a tizz as much as I was. That was the time when I most needed someone.

> She (the health visitor) wants to help, but doesn't know a lot.

> I think we didn't get enough help from the health visitors when he was a baby . . . I think anybody with a Down's syndrome baby needs a lot of help from the health visitor, especially if it was their first baby. I don't think it's available from the health visitor.

The most frequent criticisms of social workers, on the other hand were that they were unavailable and did not help:

> He (the social worker) wasn't helpful. I was coping too well, so he didn't bother. He didn't know enough, and the back-up services are poor.

> I can never get hold of her (the social worker), and when I do it's too late.

Similar criticisms are made of health visitors and social workers by families interviewed in a number of different studies (Armstrong *et al.*, 1980; Ayer and Alaszewski, 1984; Cunningham *et al.*, 1982; Ineichen, 1986; Pahl and Quine, 1984). They were said to lack specialised knowledge. Families also criticised the rapid turnover of staff, and, in the case of social workers, families felt that they were not visited sufficiently often:

> The social services don't tell you what you're entitled to. So you don't know if you're getting what you should be getting unless you inquire. If they told you more, then you'd know whether you were satisfied with what they are doing.

It is clear from the comments above that there were four main criteria used by mothers to evaluate the services of the professionals with whom they came in contact. These reflected need and varied depending on the perceived role of the professional, although some were common to all. The first criterion is the professional's attitude to the child — whether it was positive and hopeful, or negative and pessimistic. This criterion was particularly relevant for those professionals with whom parents had dealings soon after the birth of the child, i.e. the paediatrician and the genetic counsellor, and seemed to be applied to the medical profession particularly.

To some extent, this first criterion reflects the parents' need to establish positive feelings about themselves and the child soon after the birth. Pessimistic views expressed by professionals and embarrassed or unsympathetic interactions with them, are often perceived by parents as reflecting a lack of concern and a negative evaluation of the child. Since parents are often sorting out both their feelings about the child and their own feelings of worth in the early stages of adaptation, such interactions can damage their self-esteem even further and inhibit adaptation (Cunningham and Davis, 1985b). This issue is discussed in Chapter 8 with regard to the way in which parents are first told that their child has Down's syndrome and the subsequent support they are offered.

The second criterion is whether or not the professional actually met the mothers' perceptions of their needs and their children's needs. This applied particularly to those professionals who were seen as having a specific teaching or advisory role, i.e. the speech therapist, the physiotherapist, the home teacher and the psychologist. The third criterion is whether or not the professional involved the mother and showed respect to her, treating her as a competent individual who knew about her child. Again, this applied particularly to those professionals who were seen as having skills that they could impart to parents, i.e. speech therapists, physiotherapists, home teachers and psychologists.

The fourth criterion is the extent to which the professional liaised effectively with other services and agencies. This criterion was applied particularly to social workers and health visitors. Our impression was that these professionals, at their most effective, seemed to be acting as the 'named person' recommended by the Warnock Report (DES, 1978). They were well-known to the families and the acted as a link between the families and other agencies and services. That such a link is necessary is indicated by the fact that although satisfaction with individual professionals was high (Table 7.2), 52 per cent of families still had needs that they felt were not being met by services in general.

There was some confusion as to the roles of health visitors and social workers and what was seen as overlap between their roles. Reid (1983) reported that almost half of the parents in his survey nominated the social worker for the role of 'link person', with twelve per cent nominating the health visitor. Proportions were similar in this study. Eleven per cent of those mothers who had contact with a health visitor made positive comments about their role as co-ordinators between them and other services. Thirty-six per cent of those who had contact with a social worker commented positively about this aspect of their role. However, as many more of the families in the cohort had contact with a health visitor than with a social worker (62 per cent vs 35 per cent), it is not clear which professional is the more likely candidate for the role of 'link person'. This may vary with the child's age. The health visitor may be appropriate for families with preschool children, especially in the child's first year (Cunningham *et al.,* 1982). Whichever professional fulfills this role, it is clear from parents' comments that, in order to be effective, they require good training, recognition by other professionals and authority (Cunningham *et al.,* 1982). It is important to remember also that for many families, it was other families of children with learning difficulties who performed some aspects of this function, i.e. informing parents about services and benefits and how to apply for these (see Chapter 6).

A final comment on mothers' evaluation of professionals is that they were not critical of generic professionals who did not know enough about Down's syndrome. They were critical, however, if those professionals were not seen to be taking the trouble to find out, and if they did not respect mothers' competence and knowledge.

Financial assistance

In this section we consider mothers' experiences of claiming benefits, and how they had heard about these. Table 7.3 presents the proportions of families who claimed, or tried to claim, three different benefits, i.e. Attendance Allowance, Family Fund and Mobility Allowance. The figures are similar to those reported

Table 7.3: Benefits claimed by families

Benefit	Received no problem	Received with problems	Claimed did not get
Attendance Allowance (day time only)	60%	6%	1%
Attendance Allowance (day and night)	27%	3%	1%
Rowntree Trust Family Fund	27%	6%	14%
Mobility Allowance	3%	2%	1%

by Ayer and Alaszewski (1984) in their survey of families of children with severe learning difficulties in Humberside. The families we interviewed were slightly more successful in receiving help from the Family Fund (27 per cent compared to 12 per cent). This is possibly because we often helped parents to present their case to the Family Fund during our visits. Where families were refused a benefit or had difficulty (i.e. they had to appeal against a decision not to issue the benefit), the reason most frequently given was that the disability was not sufficiently severe. A number of mothers (ten per cent) complained about the long wait to receive the benefit and the amount of red tape involved.

As described by Ayer and Alaszewski (1984), mothers were most likely to find out about these benefits from other parents. However, in their study, social workers and health visitors were the least-often cited source of such information. The mothers we interviewed cited health visitors as the most frequent source (after other mothers), followed by members of the early intervention team, followed by social workers.

Respite care

One way in which families may try to meet any needs of family members which may be neglected because of the child with learning difficulties is to use short-term care facilities. In this way, families can concentrate on the needs of parents and other children for brief periods, while the child is being cared for elsewhere. The child with learning difficulties can also experience a range of new situations and challenges and thus move towards greater independence. The provision of this service has increased steadily, until by 1980, it was recognised as an important part of a 'whole package of services' for families of children with learning difficulties (Oswin, 1984). In certain areas, respite care is provided by short-term foster families, in some, families of children with learning difficulties may share the care of their children between them and, in other areas, residential units are used. These units may cater solely for respite care, or may have one or two places for respite care in a long-term children's home. They may be health or social services facilities, or, in some instances, are attached to special schools.

Sixty-one per cent of the families in the cohort never used such facilities, 25 per cent made informal arrangements with friends or relatives and only 14 per cent used formal short-term care facilities, mostly residential units (eight per cent) or short-term foster families (six per cent). The proportion of families using formal respite-care facilities in this study is much smaller than described by Ayer and Alaszewski (1984) or Pahl and Quine (1984) in their studies of families of children with severe learning difficulties. Approximately 50 per cent of the families they interviewed used this service. This is possibly due to the fact that the children in their studies were older and had more severe disabilities.

In our studies, families in which one or more of the siblings had health or medical problems were significantly more likely to use such facilities. When asked whether parents would like to be able to use these facilities more, 66 per cent said no. The majority of these felt that there was no need, or that they would miss the child:

> She is our family. We don't want to get rid of her. She isn't a burden.

Families of children with behaviour problems were significantly more likely to feel that they would like greater access to such facilities, as were the families of children who were less socially able:

> The others need a break from her. It's no holiday for them if she comes along.

These findings are similar to those of Carey (1982) where 31 per cent of mothers expressed a need for short-term care facilities. This indicates the importance of flexibility in service provision. Although respite care should be available for all families, the views of those who feel they do not need such a service or would miss their child too much should be respected and alternatives offered. Where families wish to use relatives or friends to look after their children, they should be supported in this. It is important that parents' concerns about missing their children and the children missing them are acknowledged and eased (Oswin, 1984). Finally, as long as respite care is seen in a negative way as reducing the burden of care, some parents will be reluctant to use it. However, if the positive aspects for the child with Down's syndrome are emphasised and shown to be provided, parents may be more willing to use the service (Cunningham, 1987).

Summary

This chapter, along with Chapter 8, describes the families' experiences of statutory support services and their views concerning these.

Families were receiving services from an average of five different professionals at the time of Study 3. There were significantly more professionals in contact with those families where the children had serious health or medical problems. This highlights the need for services to such families to be well-co-ordinated and integrated in order to avoid confusion. Families of children over five were in contact with significantly fewer professionals. It is important that those families who are closely involved with professionals in planning for their childrens' future and implementing interventions should not suddenly be cut off from such involvement when their children start school.

Although most mothers were at least reasonably satisfied with the services they received, a sizeable minority (ranging from seven per cent to 38 per cent) described particular professionals as very unhelpful. Only six per cent of families were not in contact with any helpful professional and 14 per cent were only in contact with one helpful professional. However, half of the families in the cohort felt that they had unmet service needs, both at the time of Study 3 and two years later in Study 4.

A high degree of consensus was evident in the criteria mothers used to evaluate the services provided by different professionals. The most frequently mentioned were:

(1) The professional's attitude to the child, whether it was positive and optimistic, or negative and pessimistic.
(2) Whether or not the professional met the mothers' perceptions of their needs and their childrens' needs.
(3) Whether or not the professional involved the mother and treated her as a competent individual who knew her own child.
(4) The extent to which the professional liaised effectively with other srvices.

Mothers were not critical of generic professionals who did not know enough about Down's syndrome, but were critical if they were not seen to be taking the trouble to find out. Health visitors and social workers most often fulfilled the role of 'link person' between the family and other agencies and services. It was evident from mothers' comments that, in many cases, their training was not sufficiently comprehensive in the area of learning difficulties to equip them for this role. The time allocated to this in most training courses for generic professionals occupies only a small part of the course (e.g. British Association of Social Workers, 1984; DHSS, 1980). Often, the concepts and models that are taught in training courses are out of date (Browne, 1982; Hanvey, 1981). Once a professional is qualified, there may be little time or few resources for in-service training.

Few families had difficulty claiming financial benefits. Where families were refused a benefit, the reason most frequently given was that the disability was not sufficiently severe. However, a large proportion heard about these benefits from other families of children with learning difficulties, rather than from professionals.

Only 14 per cent of families used formal, respite-care facilities. Twenty-five per cent made informal arrangements with family or friends. Families in which the siblings had health problems were more likely to use respite care. Thirty-four per cent of mothers said they would like to use formal facilities more than they did. These were more likely to be families of children who were less able or who showed many behaviour problems. Although respite-care facilities should be available to all families, it is important to respect the views of those who do not wish to use them and to offer alternatives.

In the next chapter, we continue our exploration of the role of professionals in the lives of the cohort families.

8

Professionals and Services (2)

This chapter continues to assess the impact of formal support services upon the families' lives, but adopts a different approach from Chapter 7. Instead of presenting the views of families whose children vary widely in age, information is presented from two studies that concentrated on particular events in the family life cycle: the disclosure of the diagnosis of Down's syndrome to the parents and the child's entry into school. These events represent times of potential strain and crisis for families (Wickler *et al.*, 1981), times when professionals are closely involved with the family, and can play a vital support role.

We present parents' views on the ways in which they were told that their child has Down's syndrome, and on the type and amount of information and support that they were given. A study in which a 'model' service was set up to meet parents' early needs is described. All of this information comes from Study 1: Diagnosis and early family needs.

The second event to be explored is school entry. We describe mothers' evaluation of the support they received from professionals in order to help them make decisions about their child's education. Their satisfaction with the school they chose and their relationship with the school is also discussed. This information comes from Study 2: Views about school.

Diagnosis and early family needs

When the diagnosis of Down's syndrome is first disclosed, two sets of people with the very different 'world views' described in the previous chapter are involved — the parents and the professional. For the professional, although the encounter may be worrying and difficult, it is soon over. For the parents, however, it is only the beginning and everything changes. From being ordinary parents, they change within the space of a few moments into the parents of a child with a disability. They have no choice about whether or not to accept this role. It is theirs, and will remain theirs for the remainder of their lives. The few moments which it takes to tell parents that their child has a disability are thus vitally important. It is a particularly sensitive period and the way in which they are told may affect their feelings about the child, about themselves and about professionals for a long time to come.

Once they have been told that their child has Down's syndrome, great uncertainty is created for parents about why it happened and what it means for the child and the family. They need information to help them make sense of what has happened. They need to construct new frameworks to understand the child, themselves as parents and the future of their families. They may have confused feelings, which could include resentment and rejection, but also a desire to protect the infant. They may have doubts about whether they will cope (Cunningham and Davis, 1985a). There are many ways in which this first encounter between the professionals and the parents can go wrong. If the professional gives false assurances and delays the telling, the parent may interpret this as a fear that they will not cope. By being abrupt and listing negative consequences, the professional may increase parental fears of their own negativism.

When the first 30 families in the cohort were interviewed, they complained about mothers and fathers being told separately, in an abrupt and uncaring way, often in a public place and/or without access to a private place afterwards. Most of them told after the first week complained of the delay and of false assurances given (Cunningham and Sloper, 1977a):

I would sooner have known right at the beginning.

He (the paediatrician) never told me she was mentally handicapped, just a mongol.

My sister found out from a nurse she knew.

He (the husband) didn't know until the final results were

through. I couldn't tell him, as I'm too much of a coward.

The tests all went wrong but they told my mother that they thought he was anaemic. She still doesn't accept that he's mentally handicapped.

These findings are similar to those of many other British (e.g. Berg *et al.*, 1969; Carr, 1970; Drillien and Wilkinson, 1964), and American studies (e.g. Gayton and Walker, 1974; Pueschel and Murphy, 1976).

Another interview study with parents of children in the cohort born three years later, indicated that there had been some improvements over time, (Cunningham *et al.*, 1984). Whereas in the early sample, only 30 per cent of parents had been together when they were told the diagnosis, in the later sample, the proportion told together had increased to 75 per cent. Also, the proportion of parents who were told within the first week had increased from 67 per cent to 75 per cent. There were significantly less complaints about the way they were told. Seventy-five per cent of parents felt they had been told in a sympathetic and caring way. However, 58 per cent of the later sample still expressed some form of dissatisfaction. No improvement had occurred in the arrangement of further appointments following disclosure, or in the provision of information and guidance before the family left the hospital.

When we reported the findings of parental dissatisfaction back to medical personnel, they frequently made the point that such feelings were inevitable and that anger towards the person disclosing bad news could not be avoided and may be cathartic. This did not conform with our finding in the first interview study — that those parents who felt they had been told well wanted to meet the 'teller' again. All those who felt that they had been told badly did not. In order to test the inevitability of dissatisfaction and explore more satisfactory procedures, a sample of parents were given an 'ideal service' according to the wishes that parents in the two earlier surveys had specified. The views of these parents were compared to those of a group of parents whose children had been born at the same time in other health districts (Cunningham *et al.*, 1984). Details of the methods used in this study are given in Chapter 1. The elements of the 'ideal service' were:

(1) Parents were told the diagnosis by a consultant paediatrician.

If possible, the specialist health visitor was present. They were told as soon as possible, except where the mother was ill. They were together in a private place, with no other medical personnel present and where they were unlikely to be disturbed. The infant was present and they were holding or touching the baby.

(2) They were told in a straightforward manner. An example might be:

> Hello, I am Dr. X, the baby specialist. I have been examining (child's name) and have found several features that suggest that he/she may have Down's syndrome. Do you know what that is? (pause) — it is what used to be called mongolism.

They were then given as much time as they wished to ask questions.

(3) They were told that the specialist health visitor would see them again as soon as they wished. She would visit them at home and would be able to answer their questions and give them advice and suggestions for practical things to do with the infant. Either the paediatrician or health visitor would talk to other family members if the parent wished this.

(4) The health visitor would provide a regular home-visiting service, giving advice on health and development, introducing parents to other families if they so desired and providing information on community services and literature.

Interviews by an independent researcher within six months of the birth found no dissatisfaction from parents receiving the 'ideal service' and very positive attitudes to the child and the services.

> He was very kind, told us well really, and when I was crying he picked up the baby and cuddled him while we talked.

In the comparison group, levels of criticism were similar to the earlier survey. It was concluded that anger and dissatisfaction are not inevitable reactions, and that parents' painful experiences at this time can be considerably reduced.

> To assume that the pain and anguish felt is inevitable and to interpret parental criticism as non-acceptance or projected anger is to apply a pathological model. Such models explain behaviour in terms of untreatable factors which obstruct any

search for alternative explanations and treatments and so maintain the status quo.

(Cunningham, 1984, p. 3)

Of interest, were two families in the 'ideal' group who did not receive this 'ideal service'. Changes in hospital registrars caused a break in the policy. Both of these families felt they were informed badly and failed to take the infant home. Thus, a clear policy, which is known by all personnel, should be set up and maintained. In particular, the role of nurses and midwives has to be clarified. Too often, parents complain about false assurances given by nurses that all is well. The same nurses complain that they are forced to be untruthful because of hospital policy. Ironically, many parents suspect something is wrong because of changes in the hospital routine and yet, at the same time, are reassured that all is well (Cunningham and Sloper, 1977a). This cannot provide a confident and mutually respectful relationship that is a necessary foundation for later parental adjustment. From discussions with parents, it is clear that they wish disclosures to be given by their paediatrician, obstetrician or GP, i.e. the most highly qualified person.

There is considerable information available to show how the initial disclosure and subsequent counselling might proceed, and what help parents want (Cunningham and Davis, 1985b; Fost, 1981; Quine and Pahl, 1986; Ley, 1977). Since this is a process of adjustment and adaptation that takes time, it is essential that continuity is established between hospital and community services, through a 'named person', who has counselling skills. It is vital also that recognition is given to the difficulty of the task faced by professionals who have to tell parents that their child has a disability and/or support them through this early period. Models of adaptation and counselling skills are required, and support should also be provided to enable the professional to cope with these difficulties. It is important to realise that it is often the parents who have to tell others that their child has Down's syndrome, and counselling should be provided to help them accomplish this.

The importance of early support and counselling is highlighted by mothers' comments about the early intervention service that they received. As part of Study 3: The child, the family and the community, we asked them what they liked about the intervention. For some parents, Study 3 was carried out when their children were nine years old and the active phase of the intervention had ceased over seven years previously. Ninety-nine per cent of mothers felt that the intervention had helped: 69 per cent referred to the support, reassurance and encouragement they had received, 69 per cent to the practical suggestions for helping their child and 21 per cent to the clear explanation of everything:

> It gave me the confidence to know that what I was doing was the right thing. I don't know what I would have done without it.

> You knew you weren't alone.

> Both the moral support that they gave me and that I didn't feel so isolated. It helped me a lot and I think through helping me feel better, then I could help the baby.

> They were very good because you feel terrible you know. You feel as though someone's shoved you on an island on your own and you don't know which way to go really.

In a similar study carried out while the intervention was still in progress, it was clear that parents found the provision of information about development and teaching supportive in itself when provided by an informed and sympathetic visitor (Sloper, Cunningham and Arnljotsdottir, 1983).

Views about school

When a child starts school, this marks a major transition point for the child and the parents. It is the beginning of a new stage in the family life cycle.

For the parents, this transition may mean the loss of the companionship provided by their young child, and the loss of their teaching/caring role for at least part of the day. They may feel that other forces are at work in the child — the school and the peer group. They may experience relief, a sense of freedom and of new possibilities available to them and they may feel uneasy about feeling relieved. They may feel that when their children enter school, they will be judged as parents as well as their children being judged as pupils. They will certainly have to interact in some way with the school, either directly or through the child. Continuity between home and school has been a central concern of educators for many years, and a number of studies have investigated home – school relationships (e.g. Blatchford, Battle and Mays, 1982; Cleave *et al.*, 1982). The Plowden Report (DES, 1967) emphasised:

> the importance of the role of parents and how their attitude to and interest in the education of their child appeared to be the single factor in the circumstances of the home which contributed most to the child's progress at school. (p. vii)

For parents of children with learning difficulties, the transition to school may be more difficult or confusing. They have to become familiar with the types of educational provision available, and then decide which will best meet their child's needs. This decision is not theirs alone, and they have to interact with a 'bewildering array of bureaucratic procedures' (Barton, 1986). The assessment process and the decision about which school is most appropriate may force parents once again to confront their feelings about the child's disability. At the time when they are making this very important decision, the services with which they have been familiar, i.e. health visitor, child-opportunity group, preschool, early intervention or home teacher, may be ceasing or decreasing in intensity. From being closely involved in their child's education and development, they may be unsure about what their role will be once the child starts school. Continuity between home and school may be more difficult to ensure if the child attends a special school because of distance, special transport and poor communication ability in the child.

All of the factors listed above may add to parents' anxiety at the time of transition. In order to obtain a detailed picture of parental concerns and views, we interviewed the mothers of all of those children in the cohort who were over the age of five and attending school (Study 2: Views about school). Their views are presented and discussed here. The transition to school is described first, followed by a consideration of parental involvement in, and satisfaction with, the school. Finally, mothers' views about educational integration are presented.

The transition to school

Of the 60 children whose mothers were interviewed in Study 2:

Views about school, ten per cent attended a mainstream school, eight per cent a special unit or class attached to a mainstream school, 13 per cent a school for children with moderate learning difficulties (MLD school) and 68 per cent a school for children with severe learning difficulties (SLD school). The children attending SLD schools were significantly more likely to have started at those schools before the age of four years than were those children attending other facilities. The distance the children travelled to school also varied according to the type of school, with those at SLD and MLD schools travelling further and also travelling by special bus, rather than being taken by parents.

The principle of parental choice with regard to the school their child will attend is stated in the 1981 Education Act. Section 6 states that parents have a right to express a preference for the school they wish their child to attend. Local education authorities have to comply with this preference, except where this would 'prejudice the provision of efficient education or the efficient use of resources'. Section 2(3) states that account has to be taken of the views of parents in the provision of special education.

The majority of children (68 per cent) were attending the school of their parents' choice. Five per cent of parents had had no preference, and 27 per cent (16 parents) had wanted the child to go to another school. The reasons why this fairly large group of parents did not get their choice of schools are varied. The most common reason was that educational psychologists advised parents against their choice (seven parents). Six parents were offered no choice. All of the mothers who felt they had not been given any choice, or where no alternatives had been available, expressed dissatisfaction.

The process of assessment before starting school marks the child out as different from peers and siblings. It may cause anxiety for parents, who may feel that the child is on trial and that the future may depend on his/her performance at this time. We asked mothers about the assessment procedures. Seventy-five per cent (45) of the children had been assessed at the age of school entry, the majority by educational psychologists. Of the remainder, nine mothers thought the child had not been assessed and six did not know as the child was already attending a special school and they had not been given any information about an assessment. Thirty-two parents were present during the assessment, and six were seen afterwards by the person doing the assessment. The remaining seven would have liked to be present but were not informed when the assessment was taking place.

A large proportion of mothers felt that the assessment had been unfair (42 per cent). Many of these felt that their children were not given enough opportunity to demonstrate what they could do. This complaint was much less common when the assessment took place over a period of time, rather than on just one occasion:

Yes, it was over a period of time, not just the one. Because they have their bad days, so it was good not just the once.

The main item remembered from the assessment was the recommendation for school placement. Only 18 mothers (30 per cent) altogether felt they had been given advice about school placement, detailing the different possibilities available and the advantages and disadvantages of each in the light of the child's needs. This advice came from educational psychologists mostly (14 parents), with five parents receiving advice from teachers in the child's pre-school, and one from another parent. Of those who did not receive any advice, 75 per cent would have liked to. The lack of information and advice means that the principle of parental choice is meaningless. Parents cannot make informed choices if they do not know what the possibilities are and how they compare with each other, as in this parent's case:

It would be nice if we could have had advice, but it just seemed pointless. There was no other choice. That was the biggest upsetting thing for me when he went at two (to a special school). That hit me hard. I realised he wasn't following the same course as the other children. It suddenly hit me, that is how different he is going to be, not going to the same school, and it rubbed it in, in a way.

Significantly fewer parents whose children attended SLD schools had received advice than those parents whose children were attending other facilities. If these parents had been given information and advice, they could have felt more involved in the decision on school placement and made more informed choices.

The parents in this study showed a great deal of interest in the choice of a school for their child. Fifty-seven per cent went to visit a variety of schools before the placement was decided. A further 37 per cent visited the school the child was to attend, once a decision had been made. In 38 per cent of cases, it was the parents who felt that they had been the first to start making arrangements for their children to go to their present schools.

Table 8.1: Feelings when child started school

Feelings	% of mothers
Relief	43
Anxiety	37
Missing child's presence	40
Missing teaching/caring role	15

Mothers were asked about their feelings when the child first started at school. Table 8.1 shows their responses. A considerably lower proportion reported feeling anxiety than found in studies of the parents of non-handicapped children (Hock, McKenry, Hock, Triolo and Stewart, 1980): 37 per cent compared with 62 per cent. Forty-three per cent of mothers felt relieved when their child started school, feeling that they could hand over some of their responsibilities for the child's development to qualified teachers. Often, feelings of anxiety and relief were mixed:

I felt very nervous because it was the end of one era and the beginning of another. This was the moment that we had all waited for — her starting at normal school and we felt that it was the end of all we had worked for and yet it was just the beginning of another long fight. I didn't think I was going to miss her and I did. But in another way, it was a great help for me to have her at school because I was working and I didn't have to do that long journey (to nursery) every day.

Awful! I felt so lost, even though I had Jenny (younger sibling). Because she needed me so much and I did so much for her that I just felt so lost and depressed. It depressed me for a couple of months, probably with her being my first going to school and her being handicapped. I thought, oh, she's so little.

Comparison with research on non-handicapped children suggests that such mixed feelings are common. Cleave *et al.* (1982) report a mixture of feelings composed of 'sadness, gladness and apprehension' in mothers of non-handicapped children starting school.

Parental involvement and satisfaction with school

The issue of parent involvement in their children's education has received considerable attention in recent years. Parental involvement provides a means both of linking home and school (Cyster, Clift and Battle, 1979; Wolfendale, 1983) and of continuing the close involvement parents may have had in their child's education and development through early intervention programmes (Mittler and McConachie, 1983; Pugh, 1981). The parents in the cohort had all participated in an early intervention programme for the first two years of their children's lives. Almost half of them (48 per cent) had helped in some way at their children's preschools. In this section, we describe their involvement with their children's schools and their feelings about their level of involvement.

Most of the schools (86 per cent) had Parent–Teacher Associations (PTAs), and over half of the parents attended meetings (58 per cent). A considerable number (26 per cent) were also on the PTA committees. There was no variation according to social class in attendance at meetings or being a committee member. Compared to a national sample of primary schools (Cyster *et al.*, 1979), the schools attended by cohort children were more likely to have a PTA. The percentage of parents in the cohort who were involved with the PTA was particularly high compared with a sample of parents of primary school children, where only seven per cent were members of PTA committees (Webb, 1982). A comparison between cohort parents and parents who had not received our early intervention service showed that significantly more cohort parents were members of PTA committees. This may have been an effect of the early intervention resulting in increased parental confidence about interacting with educational services. However, although involvement in PTAs was high, parents did not find these a satisfactory means for linking home and school. They felt that their main activity was fund-raising, but that their functions should have been liaison between home and school, and involvement in school policies.

The majority of mothers felt that they could go to the schools whenever they liked (95 per cent), and 85 per cent felt welcome at the schools, suggesting an open policy on the part of the schools concerned. The mothers were appreciative of the informal, friendly atmosphere of many schools, and of teachers making time to talk to parents. All of the mothers said they thought it was important for parents to keep in close touch with their child's school. The reasons most often given were: to know what the child was doing at school (50 per cent); in order that home and school could work together (40 per cent); to know how their child was progressing (22 per cent); to get to know the teacher and show interest (15 per cent); to sort out any problems (seven per cent). Sixty-six per cent of mothers thought that this was more important if the child had learning difficulties, and 64 per cent of those mothers with more than one child, felt that they had more contact with the teacher of the child with Down's syndrome:

> With his (the child with Down's syndrome) school you can feel that the teachers are really interested in him as an individual, which you don't really feel in the normal school (the sibling's school). There, your child is just one of many.

Despite the difficulties of distance, and the fact that most parents did not take their children with Down's syndrome to school, parents made a considerable effort to keep in touch with the schools. Most mothers had visited the school at least once in the last term: 18 per cent visited every week; 27 per cent visited four to six times; 47 per cent visited once to three times; and eight per cent not at all. These visits were specifically to talk to staff about the child rather than to attend school events.

The picture changes, however, when the question of parental involvement in helping at the schools is considered. Although 48 per cent of parents had helped at their child's preschool, and 47 per cent had felt that they would continue to work with their children in partnership with the schools, only 15 per cent actually helped at school. Of those who did not help, 57 per cent would have liked to, but had not been asked by the school staff (41 per cent) or felt that they should not disturb the child at school (16 per cent). Parents were more likely to help if their children attended mainstream schools (36 per cent), than if they were at SLD schools (12 per cent) or MLD schools (no parents).

There are a number of ways in which parents can work with the school, and follow up on what the child is doing at school. For 17 per cent of children, the teacher gave the mother suggestions for activities to do at home with the child at least once a week. For a further 47 per cent, this happened occasionally, and for 37 per cent it never happened. Parents received these suggestions mainly through personal contacts with the teacher, or through a home – school diary. Parents were generally committed to carrying out these activities, and only one found them impossible to carry out. Of the 22 parents who did not receive any suggestions, 17 would have liked this to happen.

We would really have liked to help him when he was younger and been given suggestions from school. Now, we've lost the enthusiasm because we didn't manage to get anything by trying.

Despite their concerns about not being involved in working with the school, 63 per cent of mothers were satisfied with the school. The major reason for dissatisfaction was lack of communication. Fifty-one per cent of those who were not satisfied cited this reason and a further 24 per cent felt that the work being done at school was inappropriate for their children. Two mothers wanted more contact with non-handicapped children, and two cited the lack of speech therapy. Only four of these mothers were so dissatisfied that they wanted their children to change schools. These children were all in SLD schools. Generally, mothers were also satisfied with the progress their children were making at school: 62 per cent were satisfied with their child's progress in every way, 27 per cent were satisfied in most areas and ten per cent were not satisfied. This did not vary significantly according to type of school, child's ability, mother's involvement in school or whether or not the school was the one the parents had wanted the child to attend. Mothers who were satisfied with the child's progress were more likely to feel generally satisfied with the school. They were also more likely to be satisfied with the school if they felt welcome there, and if they knew what the child was learning.

Educational integration

The Warnock Report (DES, 1978) and the 1981 Education Act have both brought publicity to the question of the integration of children with special needs into mainstream education. Possibly as a result of this, parents in the cohort had often discussed this question with the researchers. As part of this study, the views and concerns of mothers were sought in a more systematic way.

Those mothers whose children were attending special schools (49) were asked whether they had wanted the child to attend school with non-handicapped children. Twenty-five (51 per cent) had wanted this and the reasons why it had not come about were varied. Only one parent had approached a mainstream school that would not accept the child. Others did not think integrated provision was available for their children (19 per cent), or had been advised against it by an educational psychologist (four per cent), or felt that classes were too big in mainstream schools and there was no special help (six per cent), or, gave other reasons (ten per cent). Those 24 mothers who did not want their children to go to school with non-handicapped children were mainly worried that the child would not be able to keep up.

When asked if they thought it was a good policy to try to integrate children with learning difficulties into ordinary schools, 30 mothers thought that it was definitely a good policy, 25 thought it was with limitations and five thought it was not. The limitations specified were: the level of disability — ten mothers thought that only children with mild learning difficulties should be integrated and special units or classes provided — nine mothers supported this, whereas two mothers felt that integration was only a good policy if the children were not set apart in special classes.

Mothers' views on the advantages and disadvantages of educational integration were also sought. Their replies to a question asking what they felt these were for all children are shown in Table 8.2. Overall, they saw more advantages than disadvantages, particularly in relation to the acceptance of children with learning difficulties in society. However, they were concerned about the emphasis on work and achievement in schools, which may lead the child with learning difficulties to feel left out or frustrated. They feared that teasing may result, because the child was seen as different. However, only three children in the sample had been teased because of their disability. All of these were in the preschool at the time, and in only one case was it more than a minor problem.

Many mothers cited the lack of special teaching or help in mainstream schools as a disadvantage of integration. For 34 of the 48 children who had attended integrated preschools, no special provisions were made. Where there was extra help, this came from the usual staff, from the mothers themselves, from volunteers or from other mothers. For those children in mainstream or MLD schools, 16 out of 19 had no special provisions made for them. Most of the mothers interviewed (90 per cent), felt that special help should be available in mainstream schools. The majority thought that this should be in the form of extra teaching help in the ordinary classroom, although some felt that special classes should be attached to ordinary schools.

Table 8.2: Advantages and disadvantages of children attending mainstream schools

Advantages — children with learning difficulties	% of mothers
Leads to acceptance in society	35
Higher expectations of child	33
Behaviour more normal	30
Children learn by imitation	28
Development of speech and play	13
No advantages	7
Disadvantages — children with learning difficulties	
Not being able to keep up	47
Being teased or bullied	37
Lack of special teaching	28
No disadvantages	13
Advantages — non-handicapped children	
Acceptance of disability	88
Learning tolerance	25
No advantages	2
Disadvantages — non-handicapped children	
No disadvantages	58
May be held back	42
May learn behaviour problems	7
Disruption in class	3

Summary

This chapter describes the impact of formal support services upon the families' lives at two different events in the family life cycle. The first event occurs soon after birth, when parents are told the diagnosis of Down's syndrome, and the second occurs when the child starts school.

Two surveys of parents in the cohort revealed a high level of dissatisfaction with the way in which they had been told that their child had Down's syndrome, and with the support and counselling they received afterwards. They complained about mothers and fathers being told separately, in an abrupt and uncaring way, in a public place and/or without access to a private place afterwards. They were unhappy if they had not been told within the first week, particularly if they had been given false assurances. They were distressed if the baby was not present when they were told and they were sensitive to any implied criticism of the infant or of their own ability to cope. They also complained about the lack of follow-up after they had been told, and the poor provision of information and guidance.

From their replies, an 'ideal service' was set up in one area health authority to see if such dissatisfaction was inevitable. Parents receiving the 'ideal service' reported 100 per cent satisfaction. Those parents in a control group, who received the more traditional service, reported levels of criticism that were similar to those of the earlier surveys. It was concluded that dissatisfaction is not inevitable. It largely results from a lack of understanding of parents' needs, poor communication and counselling skills and from organisational difficulties.

The way in which the diagnosis is told to parents is vital and can influence how they feel about the child, about themselves and about professionals both in the short and long term. Each area health authority needs to set up a clear policy that is known to all professionals in the area. Key people need to be identified who are trained in counselling skills and are knowledgeable about potentially handicapping conditions. Provision should be made for follow-up sessions and home visits to provide counselling, information and advice. Parents should be introduced to a 'named person' who will provide this service and who will act as a link between them and other services, possibly easing the transitions between services that take place at different stages of the child's life.

Like all parents, the mothers in the cohort reported feeling a mixture of 'sadness, gladness and apprehension' (Cleave *et al.*, 1982) when their children started school. Although the majority of children were attending the school of their parents' choice, a substantial proportion of parents had wanted the child to go to a different school (27 per cent). The decision about which school their child should attend is a difficult one, which can cause distress and anxiety. Very few parents received advice about school placement, detailing the different possibilities available and the disadvantages and advantages of each. Many were left feeling that there was no choice. A large proportion also felt that the assessment process was unfair to the child, particularly when the assessment took place on just one occasion.

The mothers we interviewed were highly motivated to become involved in the life of the school. They wished to help their children as much as possible in their education, as they had done when they were infants and when they were at preschool. Many of them visited a number of schools before their children started at school (57 per cent). The proportion who were actively involved in PTAs was high (58 per cent) and they visited the schools regularly to discuss their child's education. However, their desire to be more closely involved in helping at school was often frustrated. Although schools, on the whole, appeared to encourage parental contact, the area of increased parental involvement in their children's education is one that requires careful consideration and planning to utilise the untapped reservoir of parental motivation that appears to exist.

Mothers generally had positive views about integration for children in this age range (i.e. infant and junior school level).

Half of the mothers whose children attended special schools would have liked them to attend school with non-handicapped children. Fifty-five of the 60 mothers interviewed thought that educational integration was a good policy, with some reservations. They were very aware of the advantages and disadvantages of integration and, in general, saw more advantages than disadvantages. They expressed concern about the lack of resources in mainstream schools to enable the schools to meet the needs of all children.

Maternal satisfaction with the schools their children attended was high and did not vary according to type of school. Where dissatisfaction was expressed, it was mainly because their desire to know more about their children's education was frustrated.

9

Conclusions and Implications

'My family and other families with a difference are both like and unlike the rest of the families on the planet. Both facts are important.' (Featherstone, 1980, p. 240). Chapters 1 to 8 have shown how families of young children with Down's syndrome differ from one another, what they have in common, and how they resemble families with non-handicapped children. In this final chapter, we summarise and draw together the main themes that have emerged.

In Chapter 1 we said that it is never possible to assume that we fully 'understand' a family. The information presented here shows how crude any generalisations about families of young children with Down's syndrome must be. For this reason, it is not possible to offer any absolute and prescriptive rules for providing services, nor would we want to do this. Restrictions in the research methods that we used also caution against definite conclusions and generalisations. The data are based on the views and perceptions of mothers of children with Down's syndrome under ten years of age. Clearly, the views of other family members are also essential, and the findings may not apply to older children or those with different special needs. The data is also not consistently longitudinal in all its aspects, which is important when investigating change over time in such a diverse group of families. Thus, the picture we have of families and their life styles can only ever be partial and must remain open to change and reinterpretation.

We feel that the strengths of the picture we present in this book lie in the representativeness of the families who participated in the research, the special long-term relationship we have with them and the comprehensiveness of the information we collected. Given this picture, our aim is to highlight some important issues. We consider the different types of needs that different families and family members may have. We describe those families who may be particularly vulnerable and in need of support. We discuss some of the ways in which their needs can be met.

Summary of findings

Two themes recur throughout the research described in this book. The first is an overwhelming impression of family 'normality', variety and strength. The families described here vary as much as do all families. It does appear to be the case that having a child with Down's syndrome as a family member is the only feature that they all possess in common. At this stage in the children's lives, there appear to be few differences between these families and families of non-handicapped children. Their strength and 'normality' is indicated by the following findings:

— the activities and friendships of the children in the cohort were very similar to those of non-handicapped children at a similar stage of development, i.e. from three to five years of age;

— relationships with siblings were excellent in the majority of families;

— the majority of mother–child relationships were characterised by their warmth, affection, enjoyment of each others' company and by mothers' recognition of their children's personality and needs. Almost all of the women we interviewed took great pride and pleasure in their children;

— there were no marked differences in the prevalence of serious difficulties in behaviour between the children with Down's syndrome and non-handicapped children of a similar developmental age. However, there were differences in the nature of the problems shown and there were also behaviours that may be specific to children with severe learning difficulties. There were no marked differences in behaviour problems between the siblings of the children with Down's syndrome and siblings of non-handicapped children;

— there were few differences in the pattern of family activities. As in all families, most housework and child-care tasks were carried out by mothers;

— only seven per cent of marital relationships in the cohort were rated as 'poor' and most women felt that their marriages had either not changed or had improved since the birth of the child with Down's syndrome;

— the majority of the women we interviewed felt that they had high levels of social support and had enough people to talk things over with.

This is not to deny that there are problems and differences, but rather to concur with Carr and Hewett (1982) when they state that their findings are: 'a testament to the ability of ordinary families to meet the challenge of bringing up a child with Down's syndrome and of coping with all the practical and emotional problems that this undeniably entails.' (p.13.)

Paradoxically perhaps, the second theme that recurs throughout the book is that of family vulnerability. In every area of family life that we examined, a small proportion of families were experiencing difficulties and restrictions in activities and relationships. Often, they were coping with extra demands and pressures. This vulnerability was expressed in a number of different ways and in response to a number of different factors. A common feature in the families was concern for the child's future. Many families adopted the strategy of living from 'day to day' and felt anxiety at being unable to anticipate the future.

One of the most striking indicators of difficulty occurred in families where the children showed high levels of behaviour problems. These had pervasive and lasting effects. Where they occurred, the children's activities were restricted and their relationships with friends and family were poor. Their mothers found behaviour problems difficult to deal with and these were often associated with maternal distress and depression. It is not possible to say to what extent the behaviour difficulties caused other difficulties or were a response to them. However, they serve as a marker that a family is distressed and in need of help.

A number of different subgroups of vulnerable families were identified:

— families of children with serious physical or health problems. These families were unable to go out as often as the majority of other families. They also had to deal with many more professionals. Some of them were coping with the knowledge that their child would not live for long;

— families of children with more severe learning difficulties. These children were likely to have difficulties in their activities and relationships with other children. They were also likely to show

high levels of behaviour problems with all the consequences of these for the child and the family;
— families who were coping with unemployment and/or poor parental education. In these families, the children also showed high levels of behaviour problems and many of the mothers felt unsupported by their extended families;
— families who had difficulty adjusting to the child and where the mother–child relationship continues to be poor. In this group of families, the child was perceived as being difficult. This constellation of factors was associated with maternal feelings of restriction, isolation and dissatisfaction and with high Malaise scores. For a small group of families, poor mother–child relationships reflected poor family relationships generally. In these families, the children were described as showing socially intrusive behaviours. Again here, it is not possible to say which factors are causal.

In the next section, we present some suggestions for preventing these difficulties and for intervening where they already exist. We discuss how services can help all families to meet the challenges they face.

Meeting family needs

Half of the women we interviewed felt that family needs were not being met by services. In their view, satisfactory service providers:
— showed positive and optimistic attitudes to their children;
— met their needs and their children's needs;
— involved parents and treated them as competent;
— liaised effectively with other services.
These are the essential characteristics of a good service as described by many reports and documents (e.g. DHSS, 1976; DES, 1978). They highlight the importance of flexibility, competence and the meeting of individual needs. Also referred to by mothers was the importance of having *a person* who was interested in them and their child, who was easy to contact, who offered practical help and emotional support and who helped them to interact with the many complex service agencies. In short, the characteristics of a 'named person' as recommended by the Court Report (DHSS, 1976) and the Warnock Report (DES, 1978). Such a 'good' service, which offers the skills of a wide range of professionals and the facilities of a wide range of settings to the family through a 'named person' should begin to operate as soon

as parents are told that their child has Down's syndrome and should be characterised by its sensitivity and continuity.

The role of the 'named person' is: to provide information, counselling and support as necessary, to involve other specialist services and professionals as necessary and to encourage and facilitate the use of ordinary, generic services. This must be accomplished while, at the same time, encouraging parental autonomy, confidence and assertiveness and respecting the boundaries of the family system. This is a difficult and demanding role and the people who offer this service deserve recognition, respect, adequate training and support.

The next four sections will describe possible aspects of this service at different stages and for different families.

Diagnosis

Throughout our contact with the cohort families, a consistent theme has emerged of the importance of the way in which the diagnosis was told to parents and the support they were offered in the first months. Time and again during different interviews, parents spontaneously return to their memories of this period. The way they are treated in this early, sensitive stage can influence how they feel about the child, about themselves and about professionals both in the short and long term. Apart from the way in which they were told, the positive characteristics they noted were, continuity and easy immediate access to a person seen as competent and caring. Again, this supports the notion of a 'named person'.

A clear policy is needed that identifies key people who are trained in counselling skills and knowledgeable about potentially handicapping conditions. All professionals in each area should be aware of this policy, so that parents can be referred without delay. Once parents have been told the diagnosis, provision should be made for follow-up sessions and home visits, to provide counselling, information and advice. Parents should be introduced to their 'named person' at this stage.

This early, sensitive and continuous service becomes even more important when we recall that one of the vulnerable groups of families were those where the mother – child relationship was poor and maternal adjustment to the child was low. Many of these families were told the diagnosis in an abrupt, insensitive manner and this may have influenced their subsequent relationships with their children. However, this is conjecture and more research is required on the characteristics of parents and families in relation to their adaptation to the diagnosis and their attachment to their child. The 'ideal' service described in Chapter 8 is only a beginning, but it is particularly relevant for that small group of families who are vulnerable in this respect.

Early services

Warm and secure parent – infant and later parent – child relationships are vital for the development of both parental and child autonomy and confidence (e.g. Londerville and Main, 1981; Main and Weston, 1981; Sroufe, 1983). Ensuring that such relationships develop may be the most important task of early services providers. Almost half of the women we interviewed expressed lasting concerns about the way they handled their children. This reflects the uncertainty that often surrounds parenting a child with learning difficulties and the fear that intuition, common sense and 'what feels right' is not enough. It is vital that professionals reassure and support parents and do nothing to undermine their feelings of competence and confidence even further by seeming to 'take over'. Parents are important advocates for their children. They need help in becoming confident in this role. There is some evidence that the parents who took part in our particular early intervention service became more assertive and active as advocates for themselves and their children. This was reflected in their significantly greater use of health facilities, mainstream preschool placements and participation in parent groups.

Most current early intervention services focus on skill-teaching and on training parents to be teachers (e.g. the Portage Approach). Although such services provide parents with useful skills, it is important that they do not interfere with the parent – child relationship or reduce parental confidence. In contrast, we feel that interventions should be 'relationship focused' (e.g. Affleck, McGrade, McQueeny and Allen, 1982). This means that attention should be paid to the quality of the parent – child relationship: the extent to which parent and child take turns in interaction and neither clash nor fail to respond, the extent to which interactions are both repetitive and yet introduce variety at a pace that suits the child and the extent to which the child can regulate both increases and decreases in parental stimulation.

Parents need to observe their children's cues closely and respond sensitively to them (Crawley and Spiker, 1983). The warmth and sensitivity of the relationship between a parent and child may be its most important characteristic.

We need to remember that the family is a system and that the sisters and brothers of the child with Down's syndrome are part of this system. Relationships with sisters and brothers were excellent in the majority of cohort families and problems appeared to be no greater, or even less frequent, than in families of non-handicapped children. This finding reflects mothers' views. It may be that children of this age do not share their concerns and fears with their parents in order to spare them further difficulties. Evidence from other studies suggests that siblings assume responsibility for the child with learning difficulties. Hart and Walters (1979), for example, found that siblings wanted to know how best to help the child with learning difficulties. The children they interviewed wanted to know more about the disabling condition, about genetic counselling, about child management and about available resources. They also wanted contact with other siblings.

Among cohort families, we found that sibling-relationship difficulties were greatest when the child with Down's syndrome was the middle or youngest child in the family. One explanation for this finding might be that children who experience the impact of the diagnosis on the family need support and guidance in order to help them to adapt. Siblings may be neglected by service providers at this time. It is important to remember that they are part of the family system and are affected by anything that affects the family.

The goal of early services has to be focused on maintaining and fostering all family members in their adaptation to the new member with Down's syndrome in a manner that is as unobtrusive as possible.

Specific needs

The service elements described above should be available to all families. Some families also have specific needs for extra services.

The families of children with serious physical or health problems constitute a vulnerable group. Many parents described finding out about these additional problems as being even more difficult to cope with than the original diagnosis of Down's syndrome:

I found she had a serious heart problem and I turned right off. I could not do anything after that. That had a dreadful effect. It was suddenly feeling that there wasn't a future.

The imparting of such news should be done without delay, in the same sensitive way as recommended for the telling of the original diagnosis.

These parents have to deal with many more professionals than other parents of children with learning difficulties. It is vital that services to these families are well co-ordinated and integrated in order to avoid confusion. Parents in this group are also more restricted in their leisure and social activities. They need child minders and respite-care providers who are as knowledgeable about their child's condition as they are. They also need to recognise the fine line between providing the care and protection their children need, while at the same time allowing them to take risks.

A second vulnerable group consists of the families whose children have more severe learning difficulties. Such children are more likely to develop behaviour problems and to be restricted in their play and activities. Their mothers are more vulnerable to the negative effects of stress, as indicated by their higher Malaise scores. Maternal responsiveness to the child's cues and consistency in management are even more important for this group of children. It is important that parents are helped to understand and interpret their children's behaviour accurately and positively. Training in methods of behaviour analysis and modification may be beneficial in some cases and could be part of the preventative support on offer. This group of mothers also indicated a particular need for respite care services. Service providers should be careful to present respite care in a positive way and should be alert to parental feelings of inadequacy or guilt at using these services.

The most vulnerable group of families appears to be those where the mother–child relationship is poor. Although some of the recommendations given in earlier sections may prevent these difficulties, services also need skills to 'restore the emotional bond'. This is an area where more research is needed to produce methods of assessing parental relationships and intervening when they are shown to be poor. It is important that parents are helped to understand their child and their child's behaviour in a more positive way. They need to understand the function that particular behaviours serve for the child and to interpret these behaviours accurately (e.g. Cunningham and Davis, 1985b). They also need to interact positively with the child and to experience some warmth and closeness (e.g. Tinbergen and Tinbergen, 1983). Then they will enjoy their child more, deal with problem behaviours more effectively, feel more competent and feel closer to the child.

In families where the child's behaviour is socially intrusive, where there are poor mother – child relationships and poor family relationships generally, it is particularly important that any intervention takes the whole family system into account. The techniques of family therapy with their focus on patterns of interaction between family members (e.g. Speed, 1984) would seem to have a lot to offer to such families. The use of such techniques with families of children with learning difficulties is explored by Berger and Foster (1986).

In many of the vulnerable families described in this section, the children showed difficulties in behaviour. As the effects of behaviour problems are so pervasive and persistent, it is vital that service providers are skilled at helping families to prevent these and to deal with them if they occur. They need to help families to observe their children accurately and to understand why the children are behaving in these ways. They need a variety of approaches for dealing with the problems, including knowing when to reassure parents that particular problems will pass and helping them to provide a family environment that encourages positive behaviours. Many of the recommendations made by Richman *et al.* (1982) are just as relevant for families of children with learning difficulties.

The final group of vulnerable families are those who must cope with the extra strain of unemployment and other adverse social factors. In these families, the children with Down's syndrome are not unaffected by this extra strain. They are more likely to develop behaviour problems, as are non-handicapped children under these circumstances (Richman *et al.*, 1982). Their mothers are also likely to lack adequate social support. With regard to these families, we can only agree with Richman *et al.* (1982) in their recommendations:

> The case for better housing, the reduction of financial strain on young families and improved employment opportunities rests mainly on the need to relieve injustice, inequality and financial disadvantage in the society in which we live. The fact that the quality of family life and of personal development of children is clearly affected by the presence of social

disadvantage provides an additional reason for political and social action in these respects. (p.203)

Continuing service needs

As children develop, the service needs of their families change. The women we interviewed were closely involved with professionals in planning for their children's future and implementing interventions before the children started preschool or school. They were highly motivated to continue this involvement and yet, their desire to be more closely involved in helping at school was often frustrated. Many were similarly dissatisfied with the advice they received about which school their child should attend and with the assessment process. Continuity of service provision is vital. When the child or the family moves from one life-cycle stage to the next, this is often a time of vulnerability. It is even more important that parents are closely involved with services at these transition stages. Continuing support from a named person could help them by reducing the distress often associated with relating painful details of family history to each new professional.

The play and relationships of the children in the cohort reflect their developmental level rather than their chronological age. This has implications both for educational and social integration. It is particularly relevant to the age of starting and finishing at mainstream play groups, nursery school and infant school. Rigid insistence on chronological-age streaming at these stages means that the children may be ignored and left out by children who are developmentally more mature or they may not be given the opportunity to do things for themselves. On the other hand, their separation at different and often distant special schools at the age of five or younger, at a time when they are moving from parallel to social play, means that they may be deprived of opportunities both to develop relationships with other children and to learn how to play and interact using them as models. It is important that these factors are considered when decisions are being made about preschool and school placement. Parents need more guidance about the assessment process and the way in which it applies to their child.

Many mothers felt that they could not let their children 'play out' without supervision either because they ran away or because there were no safe play areas. This was frustrating both for the children and their mothers, especially at weekends and during school holidays. It meant that some children were potentially isolated from other young children. There are a number of ways in which this situation could be improved. The first, as stressed by Richman *et al.* (1982) and Pringle (1980) is to increase the quality and number of supervised play areas for young children. Secondly, in school holidays particularly, supervised playschemes where young children with learning difficulties are helped to participate fully, are essential. Finally, regular stays with another family where there are young children, on a flexible and informal basis should be available for all families who wish to use this service.

Many children as they grew up showed one or two persistent behaviour problems. The most common were sleeping difficulties, which should be amenable to direct intervention, focused on child-management techniques. However, it is important that parental knowledge and experience is used to plan such interventions in partnership with professionals, and that the interventions are minimal, in order that parents' confidence is enhanced. It should also be noted that sleep problems were not viewed by all parents as difficulties. It is important that service providers focus on those concerns that parents experience and do not intervene unnecessarily.

Finally, we need to consider the implications of the fact that most housework and child care was carried out by mothers with little help from anyone else. Half of the women we interviewed said that they would like more help with these tasks and more time to themselves. Some of the provisions recommended above, i.e. playschemes and respite care, would go some way towards meeting these needs. However, this finding has broader social implications. It reflects the low status accorded to the task of bringing up children and the widespread assumption that such tasks should automatically be the woman's responsibility. A change in social attitudes towards these roles is needed to improve this situation.

Concluding comments

There are a number of ways in which further research can contribute to our understanding of the service needs of families with young children who have learning difficulties.

Firstly, the findings described here show how important it is to carry out research with representative groups of families and to follow these families through the different stages of their life cycle. The studies described in this book refer to children up to ten years of age. We need to maintain contact with families as their children reach puberty, adolescence and young adulthood. We need the perspectives of all family members, including fathers, siblings and the children with learning difficulties, in order to have a more complete and comprehensive picture of family needs.

Secondly, we need to evaluate the effectiveness of any interventions we recommend. Research studies should be set up to select subgroups of vulnerable families, to intervene to meet their specific needs and to evaluate the effectiveness of these interventions. These interventions should be tested in service settings, and the views and experiences of service providers sought. Finally, detailed and qualitatively rich studies of small numbers of families, even as small as one or two, can offer important insights that might be missed in larger-scale studies.

Many of the service recommendations made in this chapter have been made before. Some of them have been implemented in some areas of the country but not in others. All families of children with learning difficulties deserve them. When parents first learn that their child has a disability, everything changes for them and for their family. As one of the women we interviewed said: 'I'll never hit bottom as deep again'. The role of service providers is difficult, demanding and challenging. It is to remember that these families are both like and unlike other families with young children. It is to work with them to discover what the real difficulties are and then to offer the minimal, necessary intervention, at the right time, to enable them to live their lives in their way.

Bibliography

Affleck, G., McGrade, B. J., McQueeney, M. and Allen, D. (1982) 'Relationship-focused early intervention in developmental disabilities.' *Exceptional Children*, 49, 259–61

Alloway, R. and Bebbington, P. (1987) 'The buffer theory of social support — a review of the literature.' *Psychological Medicine*, 17, 91–108

Armstrong, G., Jones, G., Race, D. and Ruddock, J. (1980) 'Mentally handicapped under-fives: Leeds and Sheffield services as seen by parents.' *Evaluation Research Group, Report No 8*, University of Sheffield Evaluation Research Group, Sheffield

Ayer, S. and Alaszewski, A. (1984) *Community care and the mentally handicapped: services for mothers and their mentally handicapped children*. Croom Helm, London

Barrera, M. (1986) 'Distinctions between social support concepts, measures and models.' *American Journal of Community Psychology*, 14, 413–45

Barton, L. (1986) 'The politics of special educational needs.' *Disability, Handicap & Society*, 1, 273–90

Bayley, M. (1973) *Mental handicap and community care: a study of mentally handicapped people in Sheffield*. Routledge and Kegan Paul, London

Beckman, P. J. (1983) 'Influence of selected child characteristics on stress in families of handicapped infants.' *American Journal of Mental Deficiency*, 88, 150–6

—— (1984) 'A transactional view of stress in families of handicapped children.' In M. Lewis (ed.) *Beyond the dyad*, Plenum Press, New York

Berg, J. M., Gilderdale, S. and Way, J. (1969) 'On telling the parents of a diagnosis of mongolism.' *British Journal of Psychiatry*, 115, 1195–6

Berger, M. and Foster, M. (1986) 'Applications of family therapy theory to research and interventions with families with mentally retarded children.' In J. J. Gallagher and P. M. Vietze (eds), *Families of handicapped persons: research, programs and policy issues*. Paul H. Brookes, Baltimore

Bernard, J. (1975) *Women, wives, mothers: values and opinions*. Chicago, Aldine

Blatchford, P., Battle, S. and Mays, J. (1982) *The first transition: home to preschool*. NFER-Nelson, Windsor

Bluma, S., Shearer, M., Frohman, A. and Hilliard, J. (1976) *Portage Guide to Early Education*. Cooperative Educational Service Agency 12, Wisconsin

Booth, T. (1985) 'Labels and their consequences.' In D. Lane and B. Stratford (eds), *Current approaches to Down's syndrome*, Holt, Rinehart & Winston, New York

Bott, E. (1971) *Family and social networks*. Tavistock Publications, London

Bradshaw, J. (1980) *The Family Fund*. Routledge and Kegan Paul, London

—— Glendinning, C. and Hatch, S. (1977) 'Voluntary organisations for handicapped children: the meaning of membership.' *Child: care, health and development*, *3*, 247 – 60

───── and Lawton, D. (1978) *Tracing the causes of stress in families with a handicapped child.* University of York Publications, York

British Association of Social Workers (1984) *Evidence to the House of Commons Social Services Committee Inquiry into community care for adult mentally ill and mentally handicapped people.* British Association of Social Workers, Birmingham

Bronfenbrenner, U. (1977) 'Towards an experimental ecology of human development.' *American Psychologist*, *32*, 514 – 31

Brown, G. W. and Rutter, M. (1966) 'The measurement of family activities and relationships — a methodological study.' *Human Relations*, *19*, 241 – 63

Browne, E. (1982) 'Mental handicap: the role for social workers.' *Sheffield University Social Services Monographs, Research in Practice*, Sheffield

Burden, R. L. (1980) 'Measuring the effects of stress on mothers of handicapped infants: must depression always follow?' *Child: care, health and development*, *6*, 111 – 23

Byrne, E. and Cunningham, C. C. (1985) 'The effects of mentally handicapped children on families — a conceptual review.' *Journal of Child Psychology and Psychiatry*, *26*, 847 – 64

Carey, G. E. (1982) 'Community care — care by whom? Mentally handicapped children living at home.' *Public Health*, London, *96*, 269 – 78

Carr, J. (1970) 'Mongolism: telling the parents.' *Developmental Medicine & Child Neurology*, *12*, 213 – 21

───── (1975) 'Young children with Down's syndrome.' Institute for Research into Mental and Multiple Handicap (IRMMH) *Monograph No. 4*, Butterworth, Sevenoaks

───── and Hewett, S. (1982) 'Children with Down's syndrome growing up: a preliminary report.' *Association of Child Psychology and Psychiatry News*, Spring, 10 – 13

Central Statistical Office (1984) *Social Trends, 14.* HMSO, London

Cleave, S., Jowett, S. and Bate, M. (1982) *And so to school: a study of continuity from preschool to infant school.* NFER-Nelson, Windsor

Clements, J., Wing, L. and Dunn, G. (1986) 'Sleep problems in handicapped children: a preliminary study.' *Journal of Child Psychology and Psychiatry*, *27*, 399 – 407

Cobb, S. (1976) 'Social support as a moderator of life stress.' *Psychosomatic Medicine*, *38*, 300 – 14

───── and Jones, J. M. (1984) 'Social support, support groups, and marital relationships.' In S. Duck (ed.), *Personal relationships: Vol 5 Repairing personal relationships*, Academic Press, London

Cockburn, C. (1977) *The local state.* Pluto Press, London

Cooke, K. and Lawton, D. (1984) 'Informal support for the carers of disabled children.' *Child: care, health and development*, *10*, 67 – 79

Cowie, V. A. (1970) *A study of the early development of mongols.* Pergamon Press, London

Coyne, J. C. and Delongis, A. (1986) 'Going beyond social support: the role of social relationships in adaptation.' *Journal of Consulting and Clinical Psychology*, *54*, 454 – 60

Crawley, S. B. and Spiker, D. (1983) 'Mother–child interactions involving 2 year olds with Down's syndrome: a look at individual differences.' *Child Development, 54,* 1312–23

Crockenberg, S. (1981) 'Infant irritability, mother responsiveness and social influences on the security of infant — mother attachment.' *Child Development, 52.* 857–65

Crnic, K. A., Friedrich, W. N. and Greenberg, M. T. (1983a) 'Adaptation of families with mentally retarded children: a model of stress, coping and family ecology.' *American Journal of Mental Deficiency, 28,* 125–38

—— Greenberg, M., Ragozin, A., Robinson, N. and Basham, R. (1983b) 'Effects of stress and social support on mothers of premature and full term infants.' *Child Development, 54,* 209–17

Cunningham, C. C. (1983a) 'Early support and intervention: the HARC infant project.' In P. Mittler and H. McConachie (eds), *Parents, professionals and mentally handicapped people. Approaches to partnership,* Croom Helm, London

—— (1983b) 'Early development and its facilitation in infants with Down's syndrome.' *Final Report, Part I to DHSS*

—— (1984) 'Down's syndrome: disclosure and early family needs.' *Down's syndrome: Papers and abstracts for Professionals, 7,* 1–3

—— (1987) *Down's syndrome: an introduction for parents.* Souvenir Press (E. & A.) Ltd., London

—— Aumonier, M. and Sloper, P. (1982) 'Health visitor services for families with a Down's syndrome infant.' *Child: care, health and development, 8,* 311–26

—— and Davis, H. (1985a) 'Early parent counselling.' In M. Craft, D. J. Bicknell and S. Hollins (eds), *Mental handicap: a multidisciplinary approach (formerly Tredgold's mental retardation),* Balliere-Tindall, Eastbourne

—— and Davis, H. (1985b) *Working with parents: frameworks for collaboration.* Open University Press, Milton Keynes

—— Glenn, S. M., Wilkinson, P. and Sloper, P. (1985) 'Mental ability, symbolic play and receptive and expressive language of young children with Down's syndrome.' *Journal of Child Psychology and Psychiatry, 20,* 255–65

—— Morgan, P. A. and McGucken, R. B. (1984) 'Down's syndrome: is dissatisfaction with disclosure of diagnosis inevitable?' *Developmental Medicine & Child Neurology, 26,* 33–9

—— and Sloper, P. (1977a) 'Parents of Down's syndrome babies: their early needs.' *Child: care, health and development, 3,* 325–47

—— and Sloper, P. (1977b) 'Down's syndrome: a positive approach to parent and professional collaboration.' *Health Visitor, 50,* 32

Cyster, R., Clift, P. S. and Battle, S. (1979) *Parental involvement in primary schools.* NFER-Nelson, Windsor

Dale, P., Davies, M., Morrison, T. and Waters, J. (1986) *Dangerous families: assessment and treatment of child abuse.* Tavistock Publications, London

Darling, R. B. (1983) 'Parent–professional interaction: the roots of misunderstanding.' In M. Seligman (ed.), *The family with a handicapped child, understanding and treatment.* Grune and Stratton Inc., Orlando, Florida

Davie, C. E., Hutt, S. J., Vincent, E. and Mason, M. (1984) *The young child at home.* NFER-Nelson, Windsor

Department of Education and Science (1967) 'Children and their primary schools: a report of the Central Advisory Council for Education. *The Plowden Report,* HMSO, London

—— (1978) 'Special educational needs: report of the committee of enquiry into the education of handicapped children and young people.' *The Warnock Report, Cmnd 7212,* HMSO, London

—— (1981) *Education Act.* HMSO, London

Department of Health and Social Security (1971) 'Better services for the mentally handicapped.' *Cmnd 4683,* HMSO, London

—— (1976) Fit for the future. 'Court committee report on child health services.' *Cmnd 6684,* HMSO, London

—— (1978) Government circular LAC(78)2

—— (1980) 'A review of mental handicap services in England since the 1971 White Paper.' *Mental Handicap: Progress, Problems and Priorities,* HMSO, London

—— (1981) *Care in action: a handbook of policies and priorities for the health and social services in England.* HMSO, London

Doll, E. A. (1965) *Vineland Social Maturity Scale.* American Guidance Service, Minnesota

Drillien, C. H. and Wilkinson, E. M. (1964) 'Mongolism: when should parents be told?' *British Medical Journal, 2,* 1306 – 7

Dunn, J. and Kendrick, C. (1980) 'The arrival of a sibling. Changes in patterns of interactions between mother and first born child.' *Journal of Child Psychology and Psychiatry, 21,* 119 – 32

—— and —— (1981) 'Interaction between young siblings: Association with the interaction between mother and first born child.' *Developmental Psychology, 17,* 3, 336 – 43

Dunst, C. J., Trivette, C. M. and Cross, A. H. (1986) 'Roles and support networks of mothers of handicapped children. In R. R. Fewell and P. F. Vadasy (eds), *Families of handicapped children: needs and supports across the life span,* Pro-Ed, Austin, Texas

Featherstone, H. (1980) *A difference in the family. Life with a disabled child.* Basic Books, New York

Folkman, S., Schaefer, C. and Lazarus, R. S. (1979) 'Cognitive processes as mediators of stress and coping.' In V. Hamilton and D. W. Warburton (eds), *Human stress and cognition,* John Wiley, New York

Fost, N. (1981) 'Counselling families who have a child with a severe congenital anomaly.' *Paediatrics, 67,* 321 – 5

Friedrich, W. N. (1979) 'Predictors of the coping behaviour of mothers of handicapped children.' *Journal of Consulting and Clinical Psychology, 47,* 1140 – 1

—— and Friedrich, W. L. (1981) 'Psychosocial assets of parents of handicapped and non-handicapped children.' *American Journal of Mental Deficiency, 85,* 551 – 3

Gath, A. (1973) 'The school age siblings of mongol children.' *British Journal of Psychiatry, 123,* 161 – 7

Bibliography

———— (1978) *Down's syndrome and the family: the early years*. Academic Press, London

———— and Gumley, D. (1984) 'Down's syndrome and the family: follow-up of children first seen in infancy.' *Developmental Medicine & Child Neurology*, 26, 500-8

Gayton, W. F. and Walker, L. (1974) 'Down's syndrome: informing the parents.' *American Journal of Diseases of Children*, 127, 510-12

German, M. L. and Maisto, A. A. (1982) 'The relationship of a perceived family support system to the institutional placement of mentally retarded children.' *Education and Training of the Mentally Retarded*, 17, 17-23

Gibbs, M. V. (1984) *The applicability of temperament scales to a British sample of non-handicapped and Down's syndrome children*. Unpublished PhD thesis, University of Manchester

Gibson, D. (1978) *Down's syndrome: the psychology of mongolism*. Cambridge University Press, Cambridge

Gottlieb, B. H. (ed.) (1981) *Social networks and social support*. Sage, Beverly Hills, California

Gourash, N. (1978) 'Help seeking: A review of the literature.' *American Journal of Community Psychology*, 6, 499-517

Graham, H. (1984) *Women, health and the family*. Wheatsheaf Books Ltd, Brighton

Granovetter, M. (1973) 'The strength of weak ties.' *American Journal of Sociology*, 78, 1360-80

Grant, G. (1984) 'Appraising informal care of mentally handicapped adults in the community: problems and priorities.' *Care Networks Project*, University College of North Wales, Bangor

Gregory, S. (1970) *The deaf child and his family*. George Allen and Unwin, London

Haggerty, R. J. (1980) 'Life stress, illness and social supports.' *Developmental Medicine and Child Neurology*, 22, 391-400

Hammer, M. (1983) ' "Core" and "extended" social networks in relation to health and illness.' *Social Science and Medicine*, 17, 405-11

Hanvey, C. P. (1981) *Social Work with mentally handicapped people. Community care practice handbooks*. Heinemann Educational Books, London

Hart, D. and Walters, J. (1979) *Brothers and sisters of mentally handicapped children. Family involvement with services in Haringey*. Thomas Coram Research Unit, University of London Institute of Education

Hewett, S. (1970) *The family and the handicapped child*. Allen and Unwin, London

Hill, P. M. and McCune-Nicholich, L. (1981) 'Pretend play and patterns of cognition in Down's syndrome children.' *Child Development*, 52, 611-17

Hock, E., McKenry, P. C., Hock, M. D., Triolo, S. and Stewart, L. (1980) 'Child's entry into school: a stressful event in the lives of fathers.' *Family Relations*, 29, 476-72

Hoffman, L. (1981) *Foundations of family therapy: a conceptual framework for systems change*. Basic Books, New York

Ineichen, B. (1986) 'A job for life? The service needs of mentally handicapped people living in the community and their families.' *British Journal of Social Work*, *16*, 311 – 23

Judson, S. and Burden, R. (1980) 'Towards a tailored measure of parental attitudes: an approach to the evaluation of one aspect of intervention projects with parents of handicapped children.' *Child: care, health and development*, *6*, 47 – 55

Justice, R. S., O'Connor, G. and Warren, N. (1976) 'Problems reported by parents of mentally retarded children — who helps?' *American Journal of Mental Deficiency*, *80*, 685 – 91

Kazak, A. E. and Marvin, R. S. (1984) 'Differences, difficulties and adaptation: stress and social networks in families with a handicapped child.' *Family Relations*, *33*, 67 – 77

Kew, S. (1975) *Handicap and family crisis: a study of the siblings of handicapped children*. Pitman, London

Knussen, C. and Cunningham, C. C. (1988) 'Stress, disability and handicap.' In S. Fisher and J. Reason (eds), *Handbook of life stress, cognition and health*, John Wiley, New York

Leach, E. (1968) 'The cereal packet norm', *Guardian*, 29 January

Lewis, H., Feiring, C. and Kotsonis, M. (1984) 'The social network of the young child: a developmental perspective.' In M. Lewis (ed.), *Beyond the dyad*, Plenum Press, New York and London

Ley, P. (1977) 'Psychological studies of doctor – patient communication.' In S. Rachman (ed.), *Contributions to medical psychology, Vol I*, Pergamon Press, London

Lloyd-Bostock, S. (1976) 'Parents' experiences of official help and guidance in caring for a mentally handicapped child.' *Child: care, health and development*, *2*, 325 – 38

Londerville, S. and Main, M. (1981) 'Security of attachment, compliance and material training methods in the second year of life.' *Developmental Psychology*, *17*, 289 – 99

Longo, D. C. and Bond, L. (1984) 'Families of the handicapped child: research and practice.' *Family Relations*, *33*, 57 – 65

Lonsdale, G. (1978) 'Family life with a handicapped child: the parents speak.' *Child: care, health and development*, *4*, 99 – 120

Ludlow, J. R. and Allen, L. M. (1979) 'The effect of early intervention and pre-school stimulus on the development of the Down's syndrome child.' *Journal of Mental Deficiency Research*, *23*, 29 – 45

Main, M. and Weston, D. R. (1981) 'The quality of the toddler's relationship to mother and to father: related to conflict behaviour and the readiness to establish new relationships.' *Child Development*, *52*, 932 – 40

Malin, N. (ed.) (1987) *Reassessing Community Care (with particular reference to provision for people with mental handicap and for people with mental illness)*. Croom Helm, London

McConachie, H. (1986) *Parents and young mentally handicapped children. A review of research issues*. Croom Helm, London

McCubbin, H. I., Joy, C. B., Cauble, A. E., Comeau, J. K., Patterson, J. M. and Needle, R. H. (1980) 'Family stress and coping: a decade review.' *Journal of Marriage and the Family*, *42*, 855 – 71

Miller, S. G. (1974) 'An exploratory study of sibling relationships in families with retarded children.' (Doctoral dissertation, Columbia University), *Dissertation Abstracts International*, *35*, 2994B – 5B

Mittler, P. and McConachie, H. (eds) (1983) *Parents, professionals and mentally handicapped people: approaches to partnership.* Croom Helm, London

Newson, J. and Newson, E. (1963) *Infant care in an urban community.* Allen and Unwin, London

—— and Newson, E. (1968) *Four years old in an urban community.* Allen and Unwin, London

—— and —— (1976a) 'Parental roles and social contexts.' In M. Shipman (ed.), *The organisation and impact of social research*, Routledge and Kegan Paul, London

—— and —— (1976b) *Seven years old in the home environment.* Allen and Unwin, London

——, —— and Barnes, P. (1977) *Perspectives on school at seven years old.* Allen and Unwin, London

Nihira, K., Meyers, C. E. and Mink, I. T. (1980) 'Home environment, family adjustment and the development of mentally retarded children.' *Applied Research in Mental Retardation*, *1*, 5 – 24

Oakley, A. (1974) *The sociology of housework.* Martin Robertson, London

—— (1982) 'Conventional families.' In R. N. Rapoport, M. P. Fogarty and R. Rapoport (eds), *Families in Britain*, Routledge and Kegan Paul, London

Osborn, A. F., Butler, N. R. and Morris, A. C. (1984) *The social life of Britain's five year olds: a report of the child health and education study.* Routledge and Kegan Paul, London

Oswin, M. (1984) *They keep going away.* (A critical study of short-term residential care services for children who are mentally handicapped.) King Edward's Hospital Fund for London, London

Pahl, J. and Quine, L. (1984) *Families with mentally handicapped children: a study of stress and of services response.* Health Services Research Unit, University of Kent, Canterbury

Pearlin, L. and Schooler, C. (1978) 'The structure of coping.' *Journal of Health and Social Behaviour*, *19*, 2 – 21

Plank, M. (1982) 'Teams for mentally handicapped people: A report of an enquiry into the development of multidisciplinary teams.' *Enquiry Paper 10.* CMH (The Campaign for Mentally Handicapped People), London

Poster, M. (1978) *Critical theory of the family.* Pluto Press, London

Powell, T. H. & Ogle, P. A. (1985) *Brothers and sisters — a special part of exceptional families.* Paul H. Brookes, Baltimore

Pringle, M. K. (1980) *A fairer future for children.* National Children's Bureau, London

Pueschel, S. and Murphy, A. (1976) 'Assessment of counselling practices at the birth of a child with Down's syndrome.' *American Journal of Mental Deficiency*, *81*, 325 – 30

Pugh, G. (1981) *Parents as partners.* National Children's Bureau, London

Quine, L. (1986) 'Behaviour problems in severely mentally handicapped children.' *Psychological Medicine*, *16*, 895 – 907

—— and Pahl, J. (1985) 'Examining the causes of stress in families with severely mentally handicapped children.' *British Journal of Social Work*, 15, 501–17

———— and Pahl, J. (1986) 'First diagnosis of severe mental handicap: characteristics of unsatisfactory encounters between doctors and parents.' *Social Science Medicine*, 22, 53–62

Quinton, D., Rutter, M. and Rowlands, D. (1976) 'An evaluation of an interview assessment of marriage.' *Psychological Medicine*, 6, 577–86

Rapoport, R., Rapoport, R. N. and Strelitz, Z. (1977) *Fathers, mothers and others: towards new alliances*. Routledge and Kegan Paul, London

Rapoport, R. N., Fogarty, M. P. and Rapoport, R. (eds) (1982) *Families in Britain*. (For the British Committee on Family Research.) Routledge and Kegan Paul, London

Reid, K. (1983) 'The concept of interface related to services for handicapped families.' *Child: care, health and development*, 9, 109–18

Richman, N., Stevenson, J. and Graham, P. (1982) *Pre-school to school — a behavioural study*. Academic Press, London

Rubin, Z. and Sloman, J. (1984) 'How parents influence their children's friendships.' In M. Lewis (ed.), *Beyond the dyad*, Plenum Press, New York and London

Rutter, M., Tizard, J. and Whitmore, K. (eds) (1970) *Education, health and behaviour*, Longmans, London

Schilling, R. F., Schinke, S. P. and Kirkham, M.A. (1985) 'Coping with a handicapped child: differences between mothers and fathers.' *Social Science and Medicine*, 21, 857–63

Sherrod, L. and Singer, J. L. (1977) 'The development of make-believe play.' In J. Goldstein (ed.), *Sports, games and play*, Erlbaum, New Jersey

Simeonsson, R. J. and Bailey, D. B. (1986) 'Siblings of handicapped children.' In J. J. Gallagher and P. M. Vietze (eds) *Families of handicapped persons: research, programs and policy issues*, Paul H. Brookes, Baltimore

Sloper, P., Cunningham, C. C. and Arnljotsdottir, M. (1983) 'Parental reactions to early intervention with their Down's syndrome infants.' *Child: care, health and development*, 9, 357–76

Smith, G. F. and Berg, J. M. (1976) *Down's Anomaly*. Longmans, London

Smith, P. K. and Syddall, S. (1978) 'Play and non-play tutoring in pre-school children: is it play or tutoring which matters?' *British Journal of Educational Psychology*, 48, 315–25

Sorce, J. F. and Emde, R. N. (1982) 'The meaning of infant emotional expressions: regularities in caregiving responses in normal and Down's syndrome infants.' *Journal of Child Psychology and Psychiatry and Allied Disciplines*, 23, 145–58

Speed, B. (1984) 'Family therapy: an update.' *Association of Child Psychology and Psychiatry Newsletter*, 6, 2–14

Sroufe, L. A. (1983) 'Infant-caregiver attachment and patterns of adaptation in preschool: the roots of maladaptation and competence.' In M. Perlmutter (ed.), *Development and policy concerning children with special needs*. The Minnesota symposia on child psychology, vol 16, Lawrence Erlbaum Associates, New Jersey

Stack, C. (1975) *All our kin*. Harper, New York

Stagg, V. and Catron, T. (1986) 'Networks of social supports for parents of handicapped children.' In R. R. Fewell and P. F. Vadasy (eds), *Families of handicapped children: needs and supports across the life span*, Pro-Ed, Austin, Texas

Starker, J. (1986) 'Methodological and conceptual issues in research on social support.' *Hospital and Community Psychiatry*, 37, 485–90

Suelze, M. and Keenan, V. (1981) 'Changes in family support networks over the life cycle of mentally retarded persons.' *American Journal of Mental Deficiency*, 86, 267–74

Tinbergen, N. and Tinbergen, E. A. (1983) *'Autistic' children: new hope for a cure*. George Allen & Unwin, London

Turnbull, A. P., Summers, J. A. and Brotherson, M. J. (1986) 'Family life cycle: theoretical and empirical implications and future directions for families with mentally retarded members.' In J. J. Gallagher and P. M. Vietze (eds), *Families of handicapped persons: research, programs and policy issues*, Paul H. Brookes, Baltimore

Waisbren, S. E. (1980) 'Parents' reactions after the birth of a developmentally disabled child.' *American Journal of Mental Deficiency*, 84, 345–51

Webb, D. (1982) 'Home-school contact.' *Forum*, 24, 45–6

Wikler, L., Wasow, M. and Hatfield, E. (1981) 'Chronic sorrow revisited: parent vs professional depiction of the adjustment of parents of mentally retarded children.' *American Journal of Orthopsychiatry*, 51, 63–70

—— (1986) 'Periodic stresses in families of children with mental retardation.' *American Journal of Mental Deficiency*, 90, 703–6

Wilkin, D. (1979) *Caring for the mentally handicapped child*. Croom Helm, London

Wing, L. and Gould, J. (1978) 'Systematic recording of behaviors and skills of retarded and psychotic children.' *Journal of Autism and Childhood Schizophrenia*, 8, 79–97

Wishart, M. C., Bidder, R. T. and Gray, O. P. (1981) 'Parents' reports of family life with a developmentally delayed child.' *Child: care, health and development*, 7, 267–9

Wolfendale, S. (1983) *Special aspects of education 3: parental participation in children's development and education*. Gordon and Breach Science Publishers Inc, London

Wolfenden Committee Report (1978) *The future of voluntary organisations*. Croom Helm, London

Appendix

Statistical procedures

The findings from two different types of statistical procedures are presented in this book. Firstly, differences in frequency between subgroups of children and families are described. These consist of univariate relationships between categorical variables. Examples include: the relationship between the presence or absence of medical problems and the frequency with which the child plays outside with friends; or, the relationship between social class and parental involvement in voluntary associations. All of these relationships were examined using chi-squared tests. Only those relationships that were significant at the five per cent level or less are described in the book.

Secondly, in order to examine the factors associated with different outcomes, we carried out a series of multivariate analyses. The results of these are described in Chapters 3, 4 and 5. The mothers' scores on the Malaise Inventory indicating stress and depression, and the children's scores on the BSQ indicating frequency and severity of behaviour problems formed two outcome measures. Other outcome measures were derived by combining categorical variables to form continuous indices. These measures include: child's friends and play, sibling relationships and maternal satisfaction. The variables that were combined to form these indices are listed in Chapters 3, 4 and 5.

The analyses consisted of three stages. In the first stage, a series of univariate analyses of variance was carried out to examine the relationships between each child, parent and family characteristic as independent variables and the five outcome measures. The child, parent and family characteristics are listed in Table 3.11. With three exceptions, these have all been described in Chapter 2. The three exceptions are: family sharing, informal support and support from professionals. These variables were formed in the same way as the outcome measures, by combining all of the information from the interviews on these topics to form a continuous index. From these analyses, all relationships significant up to the ten per cent level of significance were tabulated.

The results of these univariate analyses were presented in terms of the percentage of variance of the dependent variable explained by each independent variable. As this contains a chance component related to the size of the sample and the number of categories in the predictor variable, this component was subtracted to enable comparisons to be made between the explanatory power of different variables. Those variables with the greatest explanatory power, or those that formed a meaningful cluster were used in the next stage of the analysis.

As a number of the predictor variables showed some confounding, a second-stage analysis was carried out, using two-way analyses of variance. This indicated which variable was the stronger of two confounded variables so that the lesser could be excluded from the third stage. If two variables in a multivariable analysis are confounded, the significance of either may be diminished or exaggerated.

The third and final stage of the analysis consisted of a series of multivariable analyses of variance using the predictor variables selected from stages one and two. These analyses examined the influence of each predictor variable on the outcome measures when the effects of the other variables had been controlled. The interactions between variables were also examined. The results of this stage of the analyses are described in Chapters 3, 4 and 5.

Index

adaptation 78, 89, 110, 117–18
  see also adjustment; Judson
    Self Rating Scale
adjustment
  mothers 12, 61, 72–3, 79, 84,
    121, 137
  service needs 138–40
  siblings 45, 140
  see also adaptation; Judson Self
    Rating Scale
adoption 19
attitudes, mothers
  to learning difficulties 80–1
  to themselves 81–3, 117–18
audiologist 104, 107

Behaviour Checklist (BCL) 16,
  42
behaviour difficulties 15–16, 32,
  52–6
  and child's friends and play
    43–4
  and family activities 70, 71,
    72
  and family vulnerability 136
  and marital relationship 77,
    78
  and maternal stress 83, 84
  and respite care 114
  and service needs 142, 144
  and sibling relationships 44–5
  comparison with non-
    handicapped children
    56–8, 62, 135
Behaviour Screening Questionnaire (BSQ) 53–4, 56, 58,
  61
brothers
  see siblings

cardiac specialist 104, 107
child activities 27–32, 135
  clubs 28
  favourite activities 29, 31

  see also child friends; play
child care 65, 66–9, 135, 144
child friends 15, 30, 32–8, 135,
  143
  index of 'child's friends and
    play' 26–7, 43–6,
    155–6
  see also child activities; play
child health
  see medical problems, child
    with Down's syndrome
child management 49–51, 61,
  75, 144
child social ability 19, 77–8
  see also Vineland Scale of
    Social Maturity
child social age 19, 44
  see also Vineland Scale of
    Social Maturity
Community Mental Handicap
  Teams 102
Court Report (1976) 100

developmental scores 45, 61
  see also severe learning
    difficulties
diagnosis of Down's syndrome
  12, 13, 117–21, 138–9

early intervention
  effects 15, 28, 32, 51, 112
  mothers' views 121–2
  nature 10–11, 103, 139–40
Education Act (1981) 124, 129
educational integration 14, 36,
  129–31, 143
educational psychologist 101,
  104, 105
  see also psychologist
employment status
  and behaviour difficulties
    61–2
  and family vulnerability 137,
    142

157